"During my thirty-three years in the military, many people asked me how they could improve to be the number one person in their peer group. Bruce Tulgan analyzes, provides vignettes, and summarizes for us the essence of how to be that indispensable go-to person. Do you want to be a better leader, a better performer, perhaps number one in your peer group? Read this book. Both my sons are young military officers, and I'm sending them each a copy."

—**GREG LENGYEL**, Major General, US Air Force, Retired; former Deputy Commanding General, US Joint Special Operations Command; and Vice President, Sandoval Custom Creations, Inc.

"I am tremendously impressed with Tulgan's ability to present complicated and important issues in an understandable and useful way. This is a must-read how-to guide for understanding the positive power of attitude, influence, teaming, collaboration, building professional relationships, and being a leader in developing a culture of excellence."

—**KEVIN JACOBSEN**, Brigadier General, US Air Force, Retired; former 16th Commander (Special Agent), Air Force Office of Special Investigations; and Managing Director, Ernst & Young

"This could be the most practical and immediately usable book I've ever read. Tulgan has found a way to boil down the most complicated and delicate balance inherent in saying yes and no, making commitments, and managing expectations. Mastering go-to-ism is a thing! And Tulgan just gave you the ultimate road map."

—**ERIC HUTCHERSON**, Executive Vice President and Chief Human Resources Officer, National Basketball Association

"For anybody at any level in any organization who wants to be that indispensable go-to person, read this book. In this constantly changing world, we all have to be able to rely on each other at work more than ever and the best way is for all of us to learn how to be better at serving each other. Tulgan's research-based approach will show you how to lead from wherever you are—up, down, sideways . . . and diagonal."

—**RAY BLANCHETTE**, President and CEO, TGI Fridays

"Bruce Tulgan does it again. By zeroing in on the behaviors that make the most successful people tick, he highlights the key attributes that are critical to survive *and* thrive, despite the challenges."

—**SUSAN UNVARSKY**, Vice President, US Customer Service, Prudential Financial

"*The Art of Being Indispensable at Work* is a must-read for anyone who really wants to differentiate themselves in today's workforce. Bruce Tulgan reminds us that seemingly small actions can make such a huge difference! Great concepts in a practical and pragmatic approach to becoming that 'go-to' person at work."

—**VANESSA BOULOUS**, Chief Operations Officer, YMCA Retirement Fund

"*The Art of Being Indispensable at Work* is an incredible book that explains the subtle yet crucial keys to victory in the workplace. Tulgan provides step-by-step instruction on the necessary components to building relationships that drive success, as well as the answers to questions you didn't know to ask. With this guide, anyone can start building an upward spiral of real influence."

—**KYMBERLEE DWINELL**, Director, Global Diversity and Inclusion, Northrop Grumman Corporation

"Bruce Tulgan is absolutely spot-on about how to thrive in an environment where you have to rely on people you cannot hold directly accountable. This book provides a bona fide step-by-step plan for succeeding in today's workplace. I want everyone on my team to read it so they can learn that the key to success is serving each other, adding value in every interaction, and making themselves indispensable to each other."

—**JON MORRISON**, President, Americas, WABCO

"Finally, a book on how to be effective as an individual contributor, a team player, *and* a leader. Tulgan lays out the path to gaining influence, leveraging alignment to get things done through others, setting yourself and your team up for success, and delivering tangible results. A true lesson in servant leadership, teamwork, and followership."

—**SHAUN McCONKEY**, Chief Operating Officer, US Operations, Carclo Technical Plastics

"*The Art of Being Indispensable at Work* is practical, forward thinking, and provides excellent tips, best practices, and insights for succeeding in your career. This is a must-read for anyone wanting to be the best in their position and truly indispensable in their role. I personally plan to implement what I learned from this book."

—**ANNE ANDERTON WARREN**, Executive Vice President and Chief Human Resources Officer, MKC

"Tulgan articulates principles I've observed over the years but didn't know how to communicate effectively to others: earning 'real influence,' techniques for good decision making, the importance of professionalizing, and continually improving yourself and your work."

—**PAUL WHITE**, coauthor, *The 5 Languages of Appreciation in the Workplace*

"Bruce Tulgan provides sound insight and guidance for professionals seeking to achieve success. In *The Art of Being Indispensable at Work*, he continues his direct yet easy-to-read advice as our jobs get harder, more consuming, and require greater flexibility and teamwork. Especially amid the global coronavirus pandemic, this book is a reminder of how we need to maintain our professionalism and positivity in our daily response to challenges."

—**MICHELE McHALE**, Partner, Plante Moran

"In today's challenging economy, it may seem necessary to say yes to every request—and the requests are coming in fast and furious from all sides! Bruce Tulgan's new book, *The Art of Being Indispensable at Work*, is a practical guide to becoming the go-to person you want to be—while preserving your sanity."

—**JANET ALTMAN**, Marketing Partner, Kaufman Rossin

"Once again, Bruce Tulgan has masterfully navigated the speed and complexity of the work environment to clearly define today's top challenges and offer down-to-earth, practical advice and solutions. Using real-life examples and stories, he guides you on how to increase your influence with others, gain clarity, increase your efficiency and effectiveness, and avoid overwhelming overcommitment. This book is a must-read."

—**JILL KILROY**, Assistant Vice President, Talent Management, Horace Mann Companies

"Tulgan's message on being indispensable at work is insightful, practical, and can be applied immediately. He uses real-life scenarios to inspire us to accept accountability and take action in practicing his approach to collaboration and leadership."

—**RYAN MAYOTTE**, Director, Sales Capability, CDW

"As we recover from the economic impact of the COVID-19 pandemic, there will be challenges facing all businesses. Bruce Tulgan provides invaluable words of wisdom not only for those starting their careers but also for seasoned veterans and owners. A very good read."

—**BILL JACOBS**, Member, Board of Trustees, King's Daughters Medical Center; former owner and publisher, the *Daily Leader* and the *Prentiss Headlight*

"One of my secret weapons in building a $100 million business was figuring out how to hire and develop exactly the sort of go-to people Bruce Tulgan writes about in this book. It is an absolute must-read for business owners, management, and anyone who wants to be indispensable at work."

—**PETER STAVISKY**, founder and CEO, Barrington Media Group

"Tulgan once again delivers an extraordinary blueprint for performance that should be in the hands of every employee who wants to make a difference, get ahead, and succeed. This book is a master class on becoming indispensable that perfectly balances what to do with what not to do. Destined to become a classic."

—**PAMELA S. KACZER**, Human Resources Manager, CT Aerospace Operations, RBC Bearings

"*The Art of Being Indispensable at Work* provides practical and highly insightful answers to the top challenges business leaders and their teams face. What sets it apart are the relatable stories summarized from the decades of research Tulgan has done. This how-to guide is applicable for anyone in business who wants to become indispensable."

—**MARIA MELFA**, President and CEO, The Training Associates

"A great read. What I like most about this book is that you can feel Tulgan's passion and all the best practices are research based. Anyone at any stage in their career can benefit from more focus on increasing the value they bring to their work."

—**KEN TAYLOR**, President, Training Industry, Inc.

"Tulgan has an innate talent for explaining and illustrating how you can excel in today's workplace. No matter what position you're in or the size or age of the organization, you can use the truths expressed in this book to help you succeed, whether you're managing up or down."

—**ANISA TELWAR KAICKER**, founder and CEO, Anisa International

"In his book *The Art of Being Indispensable at Work*, Bruce Tulgan conveys valuable insights into influence and indispensability. His 'go-to-ism' credo is a significant contribution to the world of work, with actionable processes to meet or transcend every employee's highest potential, from individual contributors to C-suite executives, and everyone in between."

—**TAMMI HEATON**, Chief Operating Officer, PrideStaff

The Art of

BEING

INDISPENSABLE

AT WORK

The Art of

BEING

INDISPENSABLE

AT WORK

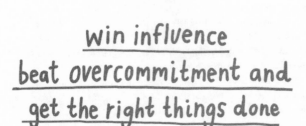

win influence
beat overcommitment and
get the right things done

BRUCE TULGAN

HARVARD BUSINESS REVIEW PRESS

BOSTON, MASSACHUSETTS

Library of Congress Cataloging-in-Publication Data

Names: Tulgan, Bruce, author.
Title: The art of being indispensable at work : win influence, beat overcommitment, and get the right things done / Bruce Tulgan.
Description: Boston, MA : Harvard Business Review Press, [2020] | Includes index.
Identifiers: LCCN 2020010127 (print) | LCCN 2020010128 (ebook) | ISBN 9781633698499 (hardcover) | ISBN 9781633698505 (ebook)
Subjects: LCSH: Executives—Psychology. | Success in business. | Influence (Psychology) | Industrial management. | Burn out (Psychology)
Classification: LCC HD38.2 .T847 2020 (print) | LCC HD38.2 (ebook) | DDC 658.4/09—dc23
LC record available at https://lccn.loc.gov/2020010127
LC ebook record available at https://lccn.loc.gov/2020010128

ISBN: 978-1-63369-849-9
eISBN: 978-1-63369-850-5

The paper used in this publication meets the requirements of the American National Standard for Permanence of Paper for Publications and Documents in Libraries and Archives Z39.48-1992.

This book is dedicated to my father,
Henry Tulgan,
the ultimate, indispensable, go-to person

Contents

Author's Note

I completed this book just weeks before the COVID-19 pandemic emerged and began killing so many, frightening all of us, and radically disrupting our world. Who could ever have imagined that such grave challenges might be just around the corner?

This book was written to help you succeed in today's increasingly demanding and uncertain world of work. It is a guide to navigating through constantly shifting priorities and unclear lines of authority. It is about how to think and conduct yourself when there are so many factors outside your control.

Well, the world just got a lot more scary and uncertain. I never anticipated this book being the *How to Win Friends and Influence People* for the postpandemic era. Nothing in it speaks, directly, to social distancing, personal protective equipment, handwashing, or even working from home or videoconferencing. Moreover, no one can predict all the many ways this generation-defining crisis will reshape our society and the workplace.

But one thing is clear: we have all just experienced, firsthand and together, how very much can change—so very quickly and with so very little warning. Now so many of our workplaces have become "virtual," organization charts are being redrawn almost by the hour, interpersonal contact has all but disappeared, and we are speaking to each other through screens. Even the most worthy, well-established missions and practices are being fundamentally challenged.

So why is this book more important than ever? Let me explain.

When everything around you spins out of control, what do you do? What *can* you do? You can control you. That's *all* you can do.

When boom goes to bust, who is still indispensable? Who will keep adding value, no matter what? Who will lead us through tough times? Who will pull more than their weight? Who will help us adapt and bounce back stronger than ever? Who will keep doing their best work very well, very fast, on time, and on budget? Who will do all this and, in the process, keep building up— rather than damaging—their working relationships?

It will be the ones I call "go-to" people. They are the people I've been studying for decades now, whose ways of thinking and conducting themselves are the basis of all the advice in this book. They are the indispensables, those upon whom you want to model yourself in the best of times—and especially in these most challenging of times.

But doing your job just got a lot more difficult and complicated. You and your colleagues, no matter where you're positioned on the organization chart, are relying on each other even more now than before. Many, after sheltering in place during the pandemic, will continue working remotely. Everybody will be under added stress for the foreseeable future, doing more with less, and tackling entirely new obstacles along the way.

Every new request will feel like a special occasion or a 911 call. You don't want to let anybody down, especially in this new, anxious world. You will want to keep proving yourself to be that indispensable go-to person.

In the postpandemic era, the would-be go-to person is at greater risk than ever before of succumbing to overcommitment syndrome. Fight it. If you try to do everything for everybody, you'll end up doing nothing for anybody.

Now more than ever, it will take extra savvy and skill to manage yourself, your many work relationships, and all the competing demands on your time and talent.

The techniques in this book were not specifically designed for the postpandemic era, but they might as well have been:

- If ever there was a time to adopt a true service mindset, this is it. The good news is that the more you serve others—by seeking to add value in every interaction—the more they want to build you up and help you out too.

- People are more likely to work things out with you, or take your word on something, when you're known for being aligned with the chain of command and you have a track record of making the right decisions.

- When you can get things done very well, very fast for people, those people will keep coming back to you.

Connection with people is the key. In the uncertainty of the postpandemic world, people will be our anchors, our relationships to one another a source of strength and security. Be a go-to person and build up your network of go-to people you know you can rely on. Invest in each other with intention. We can lift each other up and together be the jet fuel for the next great boom.

Bruce Tulgan, May 2020

The Art of
BEING
INDISPENSABLE
AT WORK

1

Fight Overcommitment Syndrome

Imagine that tomorrow morning, some high-priced workplace consultant shows up at your job. This purported expert on employee performance—some guy like me—is there to conduct a talent review: an assessment of all the personnel in the organization, including you.

Who is indispensable at work?

Who is notably dispensable?

Who are all the people in between?

What makes it harder for employees to succeed in their jobs?

What would this expert say about *you*?

If you are like most people, that last question might make you pause. Not because you're not great at your job, but because these days, doing your job is a lot harder, requiring way more than it once did.

You collaborate with lots more people than ever before. Not just those working alongside you, but all over the organization chart—up, down, sideways, and diagonal. It might be a onetime thing out of the blue, or maybe it is every so often. Some become regulars. Many you know only by email. Others you see in meetings or hear their voice on a call.

In addition to your direct boss and immediate teammates, you probably serve a seemingly unlimited number of "internal customers" at work. You are inundated by requests for help from colleagues, many of whom you might not even know. Other times, it's *you* who needs to rely on your colleagues, and the tables turn: suddenly you're the internal customer making a request of someone—often someone you cannot easily hold accountable.

At some point, this state of affairs provokes you and your colleagues to utter (at least to yourself) one or both of the most common mantras heard in today's workplace:

"You are not my boss."

"That's not my job."

But the truth is, you and most of your colleagues do want to be able to depend on each other and deliver for each other. Most everybody wants to be that indispensable go-to person. But nobody can do everything for everybody without succumbing to overcommitment syndrome, which makes it nearly impossible for anybody to consider you truly dependable, much less indispensable.

It's the irony of ironies: the so-called go-to person becomes anything *but* that. Overcommitment gets in the way. The process of trying to become indispensable too often means stretching oneself beyond human capacity so that priorities become muddled. Important tasks are left undone or done ineffectively. All of this might leave you wondering when all this collaboration business is going to blow over so that you can get back to doing your real job.

I have news for you: this *is* your real job now. Navigating collaborative relationships is not going away. And doing that job very, very well is how true go-to people, in the real world, *win real influence*, *beat overcommitment*, and *get the right things done.*

That's the art of being—more or less—indispensable at work. This book will show you how.

Welcome to the Collaboration Revolution

How did we get here? How did the ground beneath us shift from top-down management—with unambiguous orders coming from a clearly labeled boss—to collaborative work that slip-slides into our jobs from somewhere up there, down here, or way over there? To understand the answer, let's step back in time for a moment.

When I founded RainmakerThinking in 1993, companies began inviting me to speak at their conferences, train their managers, observe their operations, interview their leaders, and conduct focus groups and interviews with their employees. That work has given me the opportunity to ask hundreds of thousands of people (we lost count at a half-million), in organizations of all shapes and sizes, some version of the same basic question: *What challenges are you facing that make it harder for you to do your job and get things done?*

For more than a quarter century, the answers I've heard to that question have sounded remarkably similar. It seems that the same basic things that challenged people in 1993 are what they continue to grapple with now. From the beginning, for instance, I've heard from managers about the trouble they have managing their direct reports—and from their direct reports, about the many ways their managers could do better at managing them. Here we're talking about work relationships in which the lines of authority are very clearly defined.

But even in the 1990s and early 2000s, I also heard people talking about the challenges of work situations in which authority was *not* clearly defined—the interdependent relationships of collaboration, what we later started referring to as working across silos. Yesterday and today, getting what you need from lateral colleagues is difficult, especially if they are already over-committed, since you have no easy way to hold them accountable. And juggling incoming requests from lateral colleagues is also difficult, for much the same reason.

The difference between yesterday and today is that silos made the occasional collaborative work much easier and clearer. Everybody knew who they ultimately had to answer to. Most were able to simply keep their heads down and do their jobs within their own organizational reporting line, for the most part—their own team, department, or location.

Today, that's all changed. While most employees are still organized in silos, at least on paper, their day-to-day working relationships are all over the organization chart. What I hear—from people at all levels in all sorts of organizations and industries—is that the biggest workplace challenge is collaborating with so many people in so many nebulous relationships. The speed and complexity of work requires so many more interactions with people up, down, sideways, and diagonal that what used to be fairly easy to manage has become very difficult for most mere mortals.

Let's say you work in sales at a company that makes heavy machinery. Your job isn't just to convince prospective customers to buy a machine so you can make your sales numbers and please your boss. You are also managing a customer-order specialist to make sure the order gets booked. And maybe you're dealing with warehouse staff to make sure there's a machine in the warehouse that's ready to ship, and you're talking to a shipping clerk to make sure the machine gets on the truck. Then you might want to double-check to make sure a service technician will be in place to meet the delivery truck and install the machine.

That's when things go smoothly. When they don't—when there are no machines in the warehouse, for example, and after many weeks your customer is still waiting for the delivery— you start talking with manufacturing to see why inventory isn't keeping up with demand. Then you need to talk to someone in accounts payable to make sure your customer doesn't get billed until the machine has been installed successfully. Meanwhile, research and development wants to talk with you to get your customers' insights for future product improvements. Service wants to talk with you about your promising too much in the warranty package. Accounting needs you to get your expense reports in on time. And IT needs to make a change on your laptop.

In today's workplace, even when things go well, the number of interactions required up, down, sideways, and diagonal—for what once was a simple transaction—would make anyone's brain go on tilt. If you're that heavy-machinery salesperson, you might well ask how you're supposed to find the time to do your job, selling machines.

That is what's on everybody's mind. Everybody at work is your "customer" now. And you are theirs. Up, down, sideways, and diagonal. That's because collaboration is the latest revolution sweeping across the workplace. It is called by many names, some newfangled:

Interdependency

Lateral cooperation

Self-managed project teams

Cross-functional coordination

Dotted-line reporting

Matrixed management

Of course, collaboration itself is not revolutionary. Collaboration is as old as human civilization. As long as people have been working together, it has always made sense for people on the same team to back each other up and help each other out. When people can draw on each other's expertise and experience, they tend to come up with smarter, faster, and better solutions together. That was true when ancient humans were hunting gazelles and wildebeest, and it's been true, for the most part, ever since.

In today's context, the "collaboration revolution" is just a fancy way of describing the need for more and more people to work more and more closely together, more and more regularly, at all levels, in support of each other.

So that—in a nutshell—is what's happened. You might be wondering why.

Why Is All This Happening Now?

Some say all this new collaboration is nothing more than good old-fashioned teamwork—at a much-heightened scope, frequency, and intensity—brought about by technology, globalization, and decades of restructuring and reengineering.

That's largely true. But let's drill down.

First, there's the macroeconomic situation: today's world is more highly interconnected, knowledge driven, and fiercely competitive. In ways that are unprecedented in history, even very small organizations are plugged into global networks of potential vendors, partners, and customers.

Second, while it's true that employers continue to restructure and reengineer for speed and flexibility as work becomes more complex, the result is more dramatic than simply heightened teamwork. Layers of management have been eliminated. Managers are now handed a wide expanse of control in which reporting relationships change with the wind. Meantime, most employees find themselves in short-term project teams on top of their regular jobs. In short, everybody's trying to do more and more while leveraging the same limited resources they've always had.

My client and dear friend Geoffrey Crouse puts it this way: "Companies today need to be the best at many things in order to compete and win." Geoff is a go-to person extraordinaire and CEO of a leading laser company with operations worldwide. He told me recently that things are changing so quickly—customer needs, competitive threats, regulations, trade laws—that it's a full-time job just to orchestrate coordinated responses that jibe with the company strategy.

That's why, Geoff says, effective cross-functional collaboration is a must: "Line managers can no longer manage up and down the line and expect the company to win." Instead, managers have to be accomplished tightrope walkers, managing the traditional line relationships *while* building alignment across multiple functions. "Sales needs to collaborate with product teams to get the right product to the customer," he says. "Production needs to collaborate with quality, customer service, and finance to build the right stuff that addresses customer pain points."

What Does It All Mean?

What Geoff is describing is wholesale collaboration within the organization, as far down the chain of command as possible. The goal? To speed up and improve information exchange, decision making, planning, resource sharing, and execution—at every level of the organization—and to reduce unnecessary problems and waste. Such work environments—no longer hypothetical or futuristic, but alive and well—require everybody to deal directly with anybody and everybody, every step of the way, even though they don't report to each other or, for the most part, to each other's boss.

Think about corporate departments that provide shared services to every other department. Think of IT: everybody in every department relies on IT to fix a computer problem, even though IT doesn't report up to those other departments. Or think of payroll: if you have a problem with your paycheck, you need to get payroll to work it out for you, even though none of the payroll people report to you or your boss. Or think of building maintenance: If the toilet is overflowing, who do you call? Or think about security, human resources, finance, legal, shipping, or receiving.

We Are All in Shared Services Now

Whatever your role, wherever you work—in a restaurant, store, bank, accounting firm, hospital, school, construction site, or battlefield—your job is shared services. And so is just about everybody else's.

More and more, to get your own job done, you and everyone else will be forced to manage directly many more working relationships than before, with a much wider range of colleagues in a much greater diversity of positions, many without clear lines of authority: up, down, sideways, and diagonal.

There's a lot to love about the collaboration revolution. Working in shared services, putting our heads together to work through sticky problems—these things produce richer, more flexible products and services faster. So why is working this way driving everybody crazy?

The Trouble with Collaboration

As much as business leaders want to laud all of the advantages of the collaboration revolution, people at all levels are frustrated by its many side effects.

You are inundated by more and more requests.   You are drowning, more or less, in a cascade of "asks" from internal customers.

You want to be a good team player. You want the power that comes from being a go-to person, someone whom others are always trying to go to for help. And maybe you've got some ego invested in your ability to deliver for others. So, of course, you want to say yes. You know that you can't say yes to everyone and everything, but you often feel as if you can't say no either.

You might wonder: If I don't say yes, then who will? The answer might be "nobody," in which case, you might feel as if you really have no choice but to say yes. Or the answer might be "somebody else," in which case, you feel you had better say yes or risk becoming less of a go-to person, at least to this customer.

As a result, you probably often say yes when you probably should say no. Or you say yes without establishing realistic expectations and clear parameters about what you can do, when, and how. You say yes without asking the "asker" what you really need to know, such as "When?" and "How?" so that you can actually deliver your part. Or maybe you are waiting for the other person to do *their* part so you can do your part. This leaves you wondering which work to do in what order. Your immediate boss might, or might not, help you prioritize. But it all has to get done, as soon as possible.

So, at any given moment, you probably owe too many things to too many people. Juggling so many commitments, you'll soon start dropping balls. It's just a matter of time. You feel as if you are always in danger of disappointing somebody. You certainly don't want to disappoint your boss or any of the other bosses. Your lateral colleagues, with less authority to hold you accountable, are the ones whom you are most likely to disappoint.

Still, they need whatever they need from you, ASAP. And when you disappoint your colleagues by not delivering for them, this leads to delays and missed steps in their work. Maybe they go over your head to complain to your boss—or their boss complains to your boss. You are likely to hear plenty about how you've disappointed your lateral colleagues. You might be thinking, "Oh, OK, boss, should I disappoint you next time instead?"

Meanwhile, you're forced to rely more and more on people you cannot hold accountable. More frustrating still is when the shoe is on the other foot. Just like everybody else, you will eventually need to make requests of your colleagues, people who are working alongside you or in other teams, functions, and departments. But when you are forced to rely on them, it's easy to forget that your colleagues are facing the same pressures as you.

They also want to be go-to people, so they probably say yes too often and, just like you, find themselves overcommitted, scrambling to manage competing priorities. And when your colleagues drop the ball and don't deliver for you, this leads to delays and missed steps in your work. So, maybe then you go over their heads. What else are you supposed to do?

But think about it: What are *they* supposed to do? Like you, they cannot do everything for everybody.

Everything is my job (EIMJ). In one organization I know of, when the challenges of interdependency resulted in a high level of frustration, with lots of people manifesting very negative attitudes, the CEO tried to repair the situation by mandating positive attitudes for all. He initiated a companywide campaign around the slogan, "It is my job!" Suddenly, there were signs and coffee mugs and pens and other paraphernalia emblazoned with IIMJ. Very quickly, the slogan became the office joke, and a more cynical version began to circulate: EIMJ—"Everything is my job."

In my work with companies, I see a lot of people who might as well be wearing a cape with EIMJ emblazoned on it. These are would-be go-to people in the extreme who epitomize what I call the "superhero complex." The superhero at work wants to be positive and hardworking beyond the powers of mortal humans. The superhero wants to serve and impress everybody and disappoint nobody, by doing everything to the double, triple, and quadruple extent. No assignment is too much. No load is too heavy. They figure they will defy gravity.

Sadly, even the best attitude and most diligent work ethic aren't enough to keep overcommitment syndrome at bay. Nobody can work enough hours with a big-enough smile to do everything for everybody all the time.

Inundation + no accountability + EIMJ = overcommitment syndrome. This syndrome emerges when everything on your to-do list is "urgent and important" (at least, according to the people giving out the assignments and making the "asks"). New priorities are added to the list every day. Everybody is competing for limited resources, human resources, first and foremost. There is competition for your time and their time. None of you will get everything done. At some point, you are bound to let each other down. Nonetheless, you keep saying yes to each other.

As you all get more and more overcommitted, the chances of things going wrong, for all of you, start increasing. Delays become inevitable. Communications slip through the cracks.

People misunderstand each other or lose track of specifications. As more things go wrong, everybody has more delays and mistakes to deal with, so everybody's overcommitment just keeps getting worse.

Too often you're waiting to proceed on a project because Ms. Delay hasn't given you a critical piece of the puzzle. And too often you *are* Ms. Delay. Or you're waiting to complete a task because Mr. Mistake has to redo his part and get it back to you. And too often you *are* Mr. Mistake. How on earth are you going to get what you need from each other, when it feels like you're all at each other's mercy?

You can badger. You can beg. You can bully, bribe, flatter, manipulate. You can convince—or at least con. Or you can go over each other's heads. Maybe your bosses can't work it out, and they go over each other's head to the bosses' bosses. None of this does anything for your relationships, of course, and you will likely be told, "It would be so much better if you could just work it out at your level." And maybe it would be—if those relationships were not already frayed beyond repair.

Ultimately, siege mentality sets in. When you are drowning in other people's competing urgent and important priorities, and you have a hard time getting what you need from others, and it feels as if nobody is in control of these interdependent relationships, then pretty soon every interaction feels like a battle. You feel as if you are always under siege. Instead of embracing collaboration with your interdependent colleagues, you start to resist each other.

You are still forced to rely on each other, but it feels like pulling teeth, ever chasing each other down to get what you need.

You expect to be disappointed and thus become increasingly demanding. You take less time explaining and more time insisting, complaining, and blaming. Every incoming "ask" starts to feel like an attack to fend off. You become increasingly defensive. You work less to understand where others are coming from and work harder at hiding, debating, and resisting. Resentments grow. Pretty soon, "no" starts to seem like the only answer. More and more, you find yourselves thinking (or actually saying), *That's not my job! You're not my boss!*

Siege mentality, at its essence, is a response to feeling out of control. That's the paradox: if you seek to gain control by embracing and projecting siege mentality, you lose control even more. You say no to everything, but not for the right reasons. You say no because of your workload and your mindset—not based on the opportunity or the person.

The trouble is, the need to collaborate isn't going away just because you are hiding. You still need to rely on people you cannot hold accountable. You are still inundated with requests. If you try to hide, it starts to look as if you can't handle the workload, or you have a bad attitude, or both.

When you resist, you cede whatever control you could possibly have and undermine your ability to gain more control. When you resist, people won't want to work with you, give you the best projects, accommodate you, give you the benefit of the doubt, expect the best from you, or even give you their best efforts. They'll work with you only when they have no other options.

By resisting everything and everyone, you stop choosing opportunities and relationships. You miss out on great opportunities and create some bad feeling along the way. That doesn't mean you don't still have to deal with more work and more people. It just means they'll be less of your own choosing. The more you resist, the more collaboration becomes a weight (with fewer choices) dragging you down. Siege mentality is like fighting with your rescuer when you are in over your head.

Overwhelmed by overcommitment syndrome and overcome by siege mentality, some people burn out, blame the organization, and then leave. Wherever they end up, they probably will soon find themselves in a similar pickle.

Others burn out, blame the organization, but nonetheless they stay—and remain permanently stuck in siege mentality. If somehow they're able to keep their jobs, they become part of the bad attitude crowd, the *not*-go-to people—people to avoid at all costs.

Fortunately, most people bounce back from siege mentality sooner or later. Somehow they regain control of their time. Or they get a good rest, and then they want to get back in the game. Whatever the case, they realize that always saying no, no, no is not a way to be a go-to person. So, they start saying yes, yes, yes again.

But it's hard to avoid getting drawn right back into the same no-win cycle. "Yes, yes, yes" leads right back to overcommitment syndrome, which leads right back to siege mentality, which leads right back to "no, no, no."

Get Me Out of This No-Win Cycle

For most people, all these extra working relationships with all these extra people—up, down, sideways, and diagonal—mean a whole lot of extra work. It seems as if everybody needs something from somebody, all the time.

What makes these relationships especially challenging is that the lines of authority are usually unclear. Often you and your collaborators don't report to each other (or even the same person) in the ordinary chain of command, which leaves lots of room for misunderstandings, mistakes, and missed opportunities.

The situation is extremely complex, but the problem for you is simple: How do you and your interdependent colleagues get what you need from each other when no one has the authority to make it happen? You might think the answer is: "If I don't have authority, I just have to use influence."

The Trouble with Influence

"Influence"—it sounds so compelling on the surface, a source of power with heft and endurance. Conventional wisdom holds that when there's no clearly designated authority, using one's personal influence is the way to get things done, certainly to have them go your way. Influence actually may be even more potent than authority, not just a second-tier alternative as implied by the conventional wisdom.

But there's real influence, and then there's false influence. Understanding the difference is critical to succeeding in today's workplace in which lines of authority are so often unclear.

Let's start by comparing authority and influence.

Authority is official power—position power in an established hierarchy, within an organization with rules and resources. Authority gives you the power to make decisions and enforce them through control over rewards and punishments. If you have authority, then people do things for you because they're required to comply; this makes authority a highly resource-intensive enterprise because it needs monitoring and policing.

Influence, on the other hand, is less conventionally powerful than authority. It comes without position, rules, or control over rewards and punishments. Yet it is infused with unofficial power that can prove every bit as potent as the official variety, and even more so. Influence is the power that others invest in you because they want you to have it. It is a function of what other people think of you and how they feel about you.

If you have *real* influence, then people do things for you because they want to. It costs nothing because there is no enforcement required. Plus, people tend to work smarter, faster, and with a much better attitude when doing things because they want to do them.

But remember two things. First, regardless of how much influence you have, you can never ignore authority. *Somebody* is always in charge, even in organizations that are highly matrixed. Somewhere, someone is making decisions. There is a chain of command in which, wherever your place in it, you'd better be sure (step one) that you are aligned with your boss and the leadership. You need to know what's required. You must be clear about what decisions the higher-ups are making and what the priorities, ground rules, best practices, and current marching orders are. If you have direct reports, then (step two) make sure your direct reports are aligned with you and your boss and the leadership. *Before you can deal effectively with your colleagues sideways and diagonally, you must first ground yourself vertically— up and down the chain of command.*

The second thing to remember is that trying to "use" influence is fundamentally flawed if you seek to leverage real influence as defined earlier—that is, the kind of influence (and, therefore, power) you have because *others want you to have it*. Think about it. If you try to "use" your influence to get your way with colleagues, you might, for example, try to:

- Bribe your colleagues or otherwise seek to establish a quid pro quo

- Threaten to withhold support for them in the future

- Badger, bully, and/or manipulate them

- Charm and flatter or otherwise seek to ingratiate yourself with them

- Point fingers, blame, complain, or otherwise undermine them

- Go over their heads

The problem with these tactics is they are all akin to "influence peddling"—putting one form or another of pressure on people to get them to comply. They are all poor stand-ins for authority—efforts to wield rewards and punishments without official position power. They might get you what you want in the very short term or even for a while. (And, of course, there are always con men, thieves, and violent criminals who get away with using such pressure again and again.) But none of these tactics will result in people wanting to do things for you. More likely, they'll make people root *against* you, wish for your failure, or work to take away your power, not give you more.

That's why I call such tactics "false influence." Unfortunately, many people employ them in hopes of getting what they need within the free-for-all of our new world of self-managed teams and interdependence. And yes, sometimes false influence can work—for a while.

Real influence, on the other hand, fosters authentic, abiding power that enables you to succeed, regardless of how much organizational authority you might or might not have.

The Real Influence of the Go-to Person

So how do you become a person with real influence (which grows and strengthens over time) rather than false influence (which, at best, is short term)? How do you make other people *want* you to be more powerful and want you to succeed? How do you make others want to contribute to your success, make valuable use of your time, and work in smart ways on your behalf?

The answer, based on our decades of research among more than a half-million people in more than four hundred organizations with which we've worked, is simple: *serve others.* Stop focusing on what other people can do for you and focus instead on what you can do for other people. Make yourself super valuable to others. The more value you add, the more truly invested others will become in your success.

That's how you become indispensable. That's how you build up the real influence that makes you a true go-to person.

Here to Serve

I've been studying go-to people for decades now. Whenever I work with organizations, I ask everyone, "Who are your go-to people?" And I pay close attention to the individuals whom others cite most frequently and consistently.

Go-to people come in every variety and work at every level, and are found in organizations of all shapes and sizes, in every industry. There are as many different styles and stories as there are go-to people. But when I look for the common denominators, what unites them all is that they know how to make themselves valuable to others, consistently, in most every interaction, and they do so over time. So, you might think that go-to people must be the technical experts with very sharp skills for important tasks, responsibilities, and projects. And, of course, go-to people must certainly be very good at their jobs. But that's just table stakes for the go-to person, like hard work and a positive attitude.

More to the point, not all technical experts are go-to people. I've seen a zillion cases where an employee is, by far, the most technically skilled at doing their job, but nobody's first choice of somebody to go to. Perhaps they have a bad attitude and are not very good at interpersonal relations. Perhaps they just don't get enough done.

Sometimes, technical experts are annoying know-it-alls. They can be so convinced they're more qualified than everyone else, they spend too much of their time complaining and finger-pointing about everything they see wrong in the company, its management, its processes, and its personnel. Then, when they themselves fail to deliver, they can always tell you why it's somebody else's fault.

Nobody wants to work with that person. Most people would much rather go to a colleague who might be less of an expert but willing to take personal responsibility for working through obstacles and getting things done. Personal responsibility and getting things done are important qualities of go-to people. But that doesn't mean they are steamrollers who won't take no for an answer. Or sly organizational politicians who grease palms or flatter to get things done. Or rule benders who are always willing to end-run the chain of command or find a shortcut or a workaround. Yes, tenacity and creativity are important, but most people prefer to steer clear of steamrollers and slick politicians, and very few want to risk getting tangled up in unnecessary trouble.

Most people prefer instead to go to colleagues who know how to work professionally and methodically within the system, follow the rules, and stay in alignment with the chain of command. Things tend to work out so much better that way.

OK then, so far, go-to people:

- Make themselves incredibly valuable to others

- Are very good at their jobs

- Maintain a positive attitude and double down on hard work

- Take personal responsibility and get things done

- Are creative and tenacious but do things by the book and follow orders

- Do all those things consistently, in most every interaction, over time

Sometimes when I get to this point in my seminars, participants will remark, "Well, this is just the basics." Indeed, much of what makes go-to people go-to people is very much a back-to-basics approach. That's when other seminar participants might complain, "This sounds like the same old line our bosses hand us: that we need to suck it up, work harder, step up our game—and do it all with a great big smile."

And there's a lot of truth to that: the game is moving to a higher level, competition is fierce, and if you want to stay ahead, you'll have to keep raising your own game—just as the corporate overlords have been saying.

And that's when some of my seminar participants will begin a volley of objections: "What you are saying is impossible to maintain. All these extra relationships and all the extra work. Working double-time, triple-booked, missing vacations, never sleeping. It's unsustainable. There has to be a limit."

Of course, they are 1,000 percent right.

What Allows Real Go-to People to Stand the Test of Time

Why do you think there are so many would-be go-to people who don't succeed? Why are there so many wannabes, imposters, and most of all, sometimes or episodic (and sadly, even former) go-to people?

The answer takes us back to the beginning: because they want so much and try so hard to be go-to people that they fail to deal with the hard realities:

- Positive attitude, hard work, personal responsibility, and being great at your job are just table stakes.

- No matter how creative and tenacious you may be, you still have to do things by the book and follow orders.

- You cannot ever do everything for everybody. Overpromising may please people up front, but if you fail to deliver, that's all they will remember.

- You must make choices about what you are not going to do, so that you get the right things done. Making no choice is still a choice, and no choice is almost as bad as a bad choice.

- To make good choices, you must do your due diligence, the sooner the better, every step of the way.

- You can't be great at everything, so you need to build a repertoire of things you are known for consistently doing very well and very fast.

- You only get credit for the results you deliver. You get a lot more credit when you deliver on time and on spec.

- People are your number-one asset, but they are also very high maintenance, so managing relationships is mission critical.

In our training seminars when I start focusing on these hard realities, participants start nodding their heads and really listening. When I insist that I have no easy solutions or 100 percent solutions, but I do have lots of partial solutions that are very difficult to pull off, that's when they know I might have something real to offer them.

Cracking the Go-to Code

All I do in my seminars is teach frustrated would-be go-to people to imitate what the most successful go-to people actually do every day in the real world to (1) win real influence, (2) beat overcommitment, and (3) get as many of the right things done the right way as possible.

I've now shared these techniques with so many thousands of real people with such successful results that I know for sure we have cracked the code: What truly sets apart the true go-to people? How do they think? What do they do?

Is there a credo of the go-to person? Not that I know of—until now. I had to write one, so here's what it says:

- Understand and believe in *the peculiar mathematics of real influence* versus false influence. Real influence is the power you have when other people really want to do things for you, make good use of your time, and contribute to your success. The only way to build real influence is to truly believe, at your core, in the peculiar math: the more you serve others by doing the right thing for the long term, moment by moment, adding maximum value in every single interaction, the richer you become in real influence (chapter 2).

- Know what's required and what's allowed—*up and down the chain of command*—before you try to work things out at your own level. You have to go vertical before you go sideways (or diagonal): ensure alignment on priorities, ground rules, marching orders, and every next step through regular structured communication up, down, sideways, and diagonally (chapter 3).

- Know *when to say no* (and "not yet") and how to say yes. Remember, "yes" is where all the action is. Every yes is your opportunity to add value for others and build up your real influence. Don't waste your yeses. Set up every yes for success with a concrete plan—a clear sequence, timing, and ownership of all the next steps (chapter 4).

- *Work smart* by professionalizing everything you do, specializing in what you do best, and steadily expanding your repertoire of specialties. Know what you want to be known for. That means mastering best practices, repeatable solutions, and job aids (chapter 5).

- *Finish what you start.* The busier you are, the less you can afford to be a juggler. If you are always juggling, you will inevitably drop the ball. You have to be able to handle a long and diverse list of responsibilities and projects, but you have to execute one thing at a time. Keep a long to-do list and schedule. But break work into small doable chunks and find gaps in your schedule for focused execution time. You can only finish one thing at a time (chapter 6).

- Keep getting *better and better at working together.* Lift people up and they will lift you up, too. Relationships are the key, but don't focus on building relationships through politicking and personal rapport. Focus your relationship building on the work, and the work will go better. When the work goes better, the relationship will go better. How? Celebrate success with a supersonic thank-you. Channel finger-pointing into continuous improvement through after-action reviews. Plan the next collaboration by looking around the corner together (chapter 7).

- *Promote go-to-ism throughout your organization.* Be a go-to
  person. Find go-to people wherever you need them. Build
  new go-to people whenever you have the chance. That's
  how you build the upward spiral of real influence, the
  power that people give each other because they want each
  other to be powerful. Go-to-ism is *the art of being (nearly)
  indispensable at work* (chapter 8).

Go-to-ism works for people in organizations of all shapes and
sizes; whether you are higher up, lower down, or somewhere in
the middle; at a desk or on your feet. It works whether you are an
individual trying to navigate the gig economy, an organizational
leader in the collaboration revolution, or a foot soldier working
on a cross-functional team.

Now, I realize there are still some people in the workplace
who are not really into their work or trying hard to make their
mark in their current position. They would prefer to be left alone
to phone it in and collect a paycheck with as little effort as possible. If that's you, let me be very clear: this book is not for you. My
advice is to quit your job and go work for another organization,
preferably one that is not my client.

But everybody else, please read on. It all starts with understanding the peculiar mathematics of real influence.

2

The Peculiar Mathematics of Real Influence

From the way her colleagues talk about her, you might think Lisa Wolf, PhD, wears a cape, has X-ray vision, and can fly. And the best answer to most questions that arise in the emergency room where she works is simply: "Because Lisa says so." The best question: "What does Lisa think?"

Who is Lisa?

Lisa is a very experienced emergency room nurse, leader, scholar, and professor of nursing, with an array of degrees including a doctorate in nursing. She is also the director of research at the Emergency Nurses Organization. She's most definitely a technical expert, but lots of nurse leaders are technical experts. She is mission focused—her passion for patient care drives her work—but so are many other people in health care. She is very hardworking. Again, so are many others.

What's so special about Lisa?

Lisa is the ultimate go-to person. She's special because, for one thing, unlike many professionals in the perpetually under-staffed, high-stakes, complex world of emergency medicine, Lisa never runs around trying to do everything for everybody. Instead, she's deliberate and methodical about every interaction, every decision, and every action along the way.

Go-to people like Lisa are not mythic characters. Everywhere I go, I find them in the real world doing real jobs. They may be waiters, cooks, and managers in restaurants; farmers, truckers, and retail clerks; landscapers and ditchdiggers; engineers and factory workers; miners and heavy machine operators; bankers, doctors, lawyers, architects, and accountants; soldiers, intelligence analysts, firefighters, and law enforcement officers; journalists, graphic artists, printers, and programmers; statisticians, sales-people, and scientists; teachers, janitors, and administrators; and on and on.

Go-to people are those who are most trusted by their col-leagues to help them get their needs met on time, on spec, and in ways that improve their working relationships, or at least do not damage them. All of this adds up to what I call "real influence."

Real Influence Is the Holy Grail of the True Go-to Person

Lisa has real influence, the holy grail of the true go-to person, as a direct function of the way her colleagues think and feel about her. "What would Lisa do?" is a shorthand for solving many questions precisely because they trust her judgment. They want to work with Lisa and do things for her and make good use of her time because she is great at her job and working with her is a great experience. They want to help her gain even more power, because Lisa's power helps them get their needs met.

Real influence is not a zero-sum game:

- Its value resides in the minds of others, but it works to your benefit.

- It is completely intangible but can have enormous real-world consequences.

- It can accrue quickly and grow quickly, but it is a long-term asset.

- It's incredibly valuable, but you cannot buy it.

- People will do things for you based on it, but there is no quid pro quo involved.

- Spending it, lending it, and giving it away just makes its value grow.

- It builds and builds whenever you add value for others.

That's why I say the math is peculiar. By relentlessly adding value in service of others, you systematically build value in the thoughts and feelings of others, thereby enriching yourself and everyone you deal with, which allows you to add even more value for others. And the upward spiral of benefit is without limit.

The Long Game Is Played Moment by Moment

There is a crucial lesson that Lisa emphasizes to all of her nursing students: "Before you do anything else, check: Does the patient have an airway? Is there adequate circulation? If those things aren't there, none of the other issues are going to matter."

That is not just good emergency medical practice. It's also a great metaphor for one of the most important rules of go-to-ism: play the long game with people to build real influence, but remember that the long game is played moment by moment by doing the right thing in one short-term interaction after another.

When it comes to winning the trust and confidence of colleagues, Lisa says, "You have to play the long game. Over time, you get a reputation for making good decisions and not just getting things done, but getting the right things done and getting them done right. When you say no," she adds, "people know it's not because you don't feel like doing it, or because you are overwhelmed, but because there are good reasons. Likewise, when you say yes, people know they can count on you to follow through."

Here's the formula for the long game:

(Do the right thing moment by moment) ×

Over time = Real influence

The long game of real influence is a generous, other-centered focus based on adding value in every single interaction. And, in turn, the value you add:

- Makes the other person more valuable, including *to you*, instantly and over time

- Contributes to more successful and fruitful interactions as well as better short- and long-term outcomes

- Builds up your reputation as a true servant to others

If you understand the mathematics of real influence—and believe in it—you can make yourself incredibly rich in a very potent source of power by dedicating yourself to serving others, moment by moment, in every interaction.

What does that look like in real life?

Be More Like Lisa

Lisa knows the rules, often better than the bosses. She is relentless about ethics, procedures, and doing the right thing, but she also cuts through unnecessary bureaucracy. She is a workhorse who always has a very long to-do list and yet isn't drowning in it because she executes on one concrete deliverable after another.

She is well regarded, but she does not seek to be "most liked" by her peers, subordinates, and bosses. Rather, she is focused on continuously improving the working relationships between and among the many people—up, down, sideways, and diagonal—who must work together on patients in emergency situations.

When "Lisa says so" that means she has vetted the available information and applied it consciously to the current situation. Lisa does not pull answers out of the air. She pulls them out of evidence-based rules, procedures, marching orders, good logic, and proven best practices.

Lisa is eager to please, but not more than she is committed to making the right decisions and taking the right actions—and helping others do the same. No matter how many things there are to do at any given moment, she always keeps three things foremost in her mind: priorities, sequence, and execution. She focuses on what's most important, in what order, and how to get it done.

People want Lisa to be more powerful because she uses the power she has, every step of the way, to help others avoid unnecessary problems down the road or around the corner, get more of the right things done right early and often, and build up their working relationships through more positive collaboration experiences and improved outcomes.

That doesn't mean that Lisa and the other go-to people I've studied are perfectly selfless saints. Rather, they have learned that true servant leadership—adding value to others in every interaction up, down, sideways, and diagonally—works. They know, to the core of their being, that their servant leadership makes things go better for everyone, including themselves. That doesn't always mean doing whatever their colleagues may need or want in the moment but, rather, being enough of a true servant leader to try to always do in the moment what they believe will ultimately make everything go better for everybody.

True go-to people, those who stand the test of time, truly believe in the peculiar mathematics of real influence: the best way

Four Tactics of Real Influence

1. *Build and draw on interpersonal influence.* Always conduct yourself in a businesslike professional manner. Be the person other people do not want to disappoint.

2. *Use the influence of specific commitments.* Establish clear ownership and timelines for concrete deliverables with checkpoints along the way.

3. *Seek to influence through rational persuasion.* Use good reasons and clear arguments, not assertions or emotions, to convince other people. That means relying on verifiable facts and solid logic.

4. *Influence by facilitating success.* Do everything possible to support and assist other people in the fulfillment of their part. What are all the things you can do to make it easier for other people to deliver?

to enrich themselves is by serving others. (See the sidebar "Four Tactics of Real Influence.")

Beware False Influence

False influence comes in many stripes, ranging from the subtle to the not so subtle.

The Outright Bribe

"I cannot count the number of times I've been offered a bribe," says Officer H of the state highway patrol, speaking during an ethics seminar with fellow officers. "And it's not just the bad guys who try it, if you know what I mean." The offers come not just from thugs but also from people who are supposed to be on his team—his fellow officers.

A surprising number of people give in to the false influence of the bribe. Cynthia, a longtime pharmaceutical sales rep, reported: "You'd be amazed at how many people are willing to look the other way. So many people will take the short-term gain, and allow others to do the same, at the expense of doing the right thing."

So, what's the correct response to a bribe? The best way to respond to any attempt at false influence is to use real-influence thinking as your guide: serve others by doing what's right in the moment, which ultimately makes everything go better for everybody.

Officer H's response is: "Reject the bribe—but don't stop there. Do not let it go. Don't just look the other way. The first time I encountered bribery, early in my career, I tried to save my fellow officer by talking him out of this ethical lapse. He seemed embarrassed and backed off immediately. But it really wasn't enough. I should have reported him. This is someone who left our department but has remained in law enforcement elsewhere. I always regretted not going to the authorities in that case. I have never made that mistake again. You want people to know that high ethical standards are part of your MO."

Would Officer H be worried about retaliation, maybe even dangerous retaliation? "I can take care of myself, of course," he says. "But in any case, you have to do your duty and enforce the law, come what may." That's because the cost of taking a bribe, or even rejecting it but looking the other way, goes far beyond one incident. As Cynthia puts it: "How can you ever trust that person? Reputation follows you wherever you go."

I learned a very simple rule from the famous US Army general, Norman Schwarzkopf: "When in doubt, do what's right." That's real influence: Never compromise on ethics, even if nobody is looking. Act as if your reputation depends upon it (it does). Make it clear that you would never do business that way. You might do the other person a huge favor by urging them to reconsider their behavior. Regardless, you should probably alert the authorities. It might not be pleasant in the moment to stand up for ethics. But remember General Schwarzkopf and do it anyway.

But What If It's Just Brownies?

Let's hope that outright bribery is rare or nonexistent in your workplace. And if it ever happens, you know what to do. Usually, though, workplace bribery comes in forms so subtle, you might even wonder if it counts as a bribe.

"Connie would bake brownies for my crew," says Andrew, a shipping and receiving quality specialist, who is a true go-to person in a large product-distribution center. "That was our cue that she had a big shipment coming in. Was that a signal that she was hoping to get her shipments through our inspections without any problems? Maybe. Nobody on my team is going to let quality issues slide for any reason. But for brownies? Obviously not. She said she was just 'expressing gratitude for our work, in advance,' but still, it was just awkward."

If you are playing the long game in every short-term interaction, what do you do? The brownies feel like sort of a bribe, but you don't want to be a jerk. For Andrew, the response came easily. "Instead of rolling my eyes, I chose to look at those brownies as a cry for help," Andrew says. "Connie shouldn't have to be worried that the incoming shipment is going to run into inspection problems. So, I went out of my way to work with her on all the things she could do—aside from baking brownies—to help all of us meet our shared goals of getting her big shipments through our incoming quality inspections. I made her a checklist corresponding to our checklist. Then I would walk her through the steps in advance every time she had a big shipment coming in. Pretty soon she had a rock-solid predelivery process, and her shipments had the highest incoming quality yields ever after."

Did Connie keep making brownies? "She did, but it was clear the brownies were authentic thanks for all the shared effort," Andrew says. "We would put the brownies in the cafeteria and write a big card in red magic marker, 'Thanks to Connie!' Give credit where credit is due for the brownies."

That's what real influence looks like. By truly serving Connie, Andrew was making everything better for everybody, including making Connie a much more effective customer of the quality inspection services and ultimately serving the mission by helping get Connie's shipments through with less delay and trouble.

Meanwhile, Andrew was building real influence with anybody who was paying attention by behaving like the kind of person whom others want to succeed and in whom others want to invest.

The Quid Pro Quo

Perhaps the most common form of false influence you will encounter in the workplace is neither so noxious as a bribe nor (mostly) innocuous as brownies, but simply reciprocal cooperation (or not) used as leverage. The counterpoint to "That's not my job" and "You are not my boss" is often "You wash my back, and I'll wash yours. Let's make a deal." After all, you want to be able to go to your colleagues when you need something from them, and they want to be able to go to you. So, maybe, when you seek help from each other, there is an implicit—or even explicit—exchange of cooperation.

At first glance, what's the problem? Indeed, a spirit of mutual cooperation is certainly an aspect of real influence. But it becomes *false* influence as soon as you treat your cooperation (or not) with colleagues as a quid pro quo: "You do *this* for me, if you want me to do *that* for you."

The true go-to person does not keep a tally sheet—real or imagined—of equivalent favors to be traded for inducing colleagues to take specific decisions or actions. If you believe in real influence, you serve others because that's what's right and that's what creates the most value for everybody, in the short term and the long term.

Gayle, an actuary who is a go-to person in a major actuarial firm, puts it very well: "I already get paid by my employer to serve you. What you are asking for, that's my job, not a favor I'm doing for you. What I'm asking of you, that's your job, not a favor you are doing for me." Gayle's response reflects the path of real influence: "People can depend on me, regardless of whether

I need something from them or because I owe them. Whether I'm going to do that for you is a business decision: What's in the best interests of the business and all the various constituents here, taking everything into account, as best I can figure?"

The Freeze-Out

Then there's the flip side of quid pro quo: the freeze-out. "There are people who will hold a grudge if you make a decision or do something they don't like," says Gayle. "They might bad-mouth you behind your back or be difficult to work with the next time the occasion arises. They'll make it clear they are not happy with you. They might be nasty or cold. They might be a lot less cooperative. They really want to make you pay for disagreeing with them or not doing what they wanted."

How does Gayle handle the freeze-out? With real-influence thinking. "You have to meet their meanness with service," says Gayle. "If someone is trying to coerce me or punish me, I'm just going to show them that I'm here to do my job for them and everyone else, as best as I possibly can. It has nothing to do with their willingness to help me. I'm still going to do my job."

She continues, "If someone is really holding out on me, then I'm going to go to somebody else, of course. But I'll still be right there for the holdouts when they need me, if and only if what they need from me is the right business decision at that time. In which case, I might even try harder to deliver for them, just to show them what professionalism looks like."

Charm, Flattery, Politicking, and Appeals to Personal Rapport

At the other end of the spectrum are colleagues who seek to charm or flatter you, or otherwise ingratiate themselves—all forms of *false* influence. Although certainly more pleasant than being nasty or revengeful, you still need to beware. Don't slip into the traps of politicking and appeals to personal rapport.

"It's inevitable that you are going to make friends at work," says Ana, an analyst in a US intelligence agency, "but it sometimes makes the working relationship harder to manage, not easier. Sometimes you make judgment calls that your 'friends' at work don't appreciate. I've had people say, 'Gee, I thought we were friends.' I've had to say, 'Sorry, but this has nothing to do with our friendship.' And then the friendship suffers. Maybe it would have been better if we weren't friends in the first place."

Charles, a business process consultant, says, "This one engineering manager, from the moment I arrived, started telling me how impressed he was with my work and insisting that I was becoming his 'favorite consultant of all time.' It didn't take long for me to realize that he was just trying to manipulate me, trying to make it personally more difficult for me to recommend cuts to his budget. It was so transparent."

He continues, "But the reason people trust me to make those decisions is exactly because I don't need you to like me and it doesn't matter if I like you. I'm going to recommend cuts to your budget, if that's the right thing to do, even if you are my best friend. If it's not the right thing to do, then I'm not going to recommend those cuts, even if I hate your guts."

As Ana puts it, "If you are known, or even suspected, to make judgment calls based on personal bias, your judgment calls are worthless."

Workplace politicking and personal rapport are not good business reasons for making decisions or taking actions in the workplace. They are complications at best and, at worst, can lead you to make the wrong decisions or take the wrong actions. In the real world, the best politics in the workplace—and the best way to protect personal relationships with coworkers—is to stay focused on the work.

Going over Your Head

"If you go over my head to my boss, that's just fine with me," says Alfredo, a material-planning manager in a mining company. "You will find that I am pretty much in lockstep with my boss. If I've got it wrong, then my boss probably has it wrong too. If not, if I am not in lockstep, then you are doing me a favor. And if my boss and I both have it wrong, then you are doing us both a favor by escalating the matter and getting it cleared up at that higher level. But most of the time, you are going to find that I am marching to the company line, exactly in lockstep with my boss. So, you can usually come directly to me and you'll get the same answer you would get from my boss." When somebody tries to go over your head, think like Alfredo. Don't get angry, apply real influence thinking and seize the opportunity to seek greater alignment with your boss and the chain of command. Revisit whatever you are doing (or not doing) in your work with this colleague who is going to your boss. Ask your boss for clear feedback and direction about exactly how to proceed in that working relationship with that colleague: what, why, how, when, and where. Maybe your boss will need to seek greater alignment with the top boss. In any case, think of your colleague going over your head as an opportunity to serve the colleague, your boss, and yourself by confirming your alignment with the boss or else realizing the need to recalibrate. The more people find you are in lockstep with your boss, the less likely they will be to go over your head.

Badgering

"I have to admit, my default strategy was badgering," recalls Henry, a scientist in a nuclear weapons research facility. "I'd call, email, text, call, email, text. Then go to their desk. Call, email, text. I learned, growing up with a lot of siblings, that the squeaky wheel gets the grease. And then I found out that was pretty irritating and wasn't having the desired effect. People were avoiding me, so I got even more squeaky for a while. Finally, someone took me aside and she said, 'You must be worried that your project is not going to get the attention from me that it deserves. What can I do to reassure you?' Then we sat down and went over the whole timeline of the project and scheduled a weekly check-in meeting to monitor each other's progress."

Whoever took Henry aside was demonstrating real-influence thinking, by responding to his badgering with a gigantic favor: instead of being so irritated by Henry that, like some of his other colleagues, she started avoiding him altogether, she read Henry's badgering as an indication he feared his project wasn't getting enough attention. This colleague took Henry's needs seriously, offered reassurance, and worked out a communication plan to give him confidence that his needs would be met in this instance.

Perhaps most valuable, this colleague demonstrated for Henry a far more professional and effective way to communicate with others and get his needs met going forward.

Henry took the cue: "Ever since then, I have tried to do something similar anytime I'm working with anybody on anything. Timelines and regular check-ins work a lot better than badgering. I've always appreciated her taking me aside like that. What a valuable lesson."

Imagine how Henry will root for that colleague's success ever after. That's how real influence works.

Finger-Pointing: Complaining, Blaming, and Undermining

Kamal, a true go-to person in a chain-restaurant company, admits, "I have definitely been that person who is blaming and complaining and pointing the finger at my colleagues. I would get so frustrated and I would call people out in meetings."

Kamal recalls speaking in a meeting and being way too harsh about a colleague. "And there she was just taking notes and asking questions the whole time," Kamal says. "She didn't get defensive or angry. She said she regarded everything I was saying as 'customer complaint data' and insisted she was determined to use that data to improve. You could just see the nods of approval and appreciation as she won everyone over around the table. Then she came to talk with me one-on-one, later. She took corrective action based on my feedback too."

He continues, "I was so impressed. We worked together for years after that and she became a role model for me. She totally changed my approach to providing critical feedback. If you think of critical feedback as a valuable service, it changes how you present it. Instead of being a relationship killer, it can really improve the working relationship."

For Kamal, that colleague's example also reshaped how he responds to criticism: "I've learned that when you genuinely take criticism seriously and with gratitude, authentically take it as a valuable service that can help you get better, you turn a potential negative into a true positive. Plus, it makes such a favorable impression on people when you respond favorably to their criticism." (See the sidebar "Mind Your Attitude.")

Reject False Influence and Foster Real-Influence Thinking as Your Guide

When you reject false influence and instead let yourself be guided by real-influence thinking—always doing what's right, in the right order, and putting service to others first—you conduct yourself in such a way that things get better, right away. And you make other people really want to rely on you and want to do things for you.

You might say, "That sounds like a very idealistic view." You might worry that somebody will try to take advantage of your service mindset and your generous value adding and, rather than thinking more highly of you, they will think you are a sucker.

And it's true. There will always be mean-spirited, selfish, self-aggrandizing, or otherwise insensitive clods. Don't worry. Most people don't respond that way, and the ones who do usually self-destruct. Until they do, you still need to work with them. So, make sure you are aligned, make good decisions, plan the work,

Mind Your Attitude

Attitude may be intangible, but it really matters. You may not be able to control your feelings, but you can certainly manage your words, tone, volume, gestures, and expressions.

Bad Attitudes

Everybody has bad days or bad moments. What kind of bad attitude are you most likely to display? If you don't know, you can bet that someone else can tell you.

The porcupine says or conveys with looks or body language, "Get away from me!"

The entangler wants everybody else to be involved in their issues. They want others to notice, listen to, and engage them around their issues, even if those issues are really not the other person's concern.

The complainer points out the negative symptoms of a situation without offering a solution based on the root cause.

The blamer points out negative symptoms, like the complainer, but points the finger at a specific individual.

The stink bomb thrower makes sarcastic (or worse) remarks, curses under their breath (or aloud), or even makes loud gestures such as slamming doors or yelling.

Once you recognize yourself at your worst, you'll be better prepared to avoid that behavior and take corrective action more swiftly when it does happen. Replace the negative be-havior with one of the following good-attitude behaviors.

Good Attitudes

Even if you have bad moments or bad days, of course you have plenty of good attitude in you. Again, it's important to know what that looks like. When you are at your best, what kinds of behaviors do you often display?

You're professional. You are approachable and wel-coming, and you communicate in a highly purposeful manner—brief, straightforward, and efficient.

You're persuasive. You choose your arguments carefully, and make your arguments based on clear evidence, rather than assertions of opinion.

You're a troubleshooter. You focus on what steps you can take yourself to make things better.

You're optimistic. You project hopeful confidence about successful outcomes or positive aspects of not fully suc-cessful outcomes.

You're generous. You offer your respect, commitment, hard work, creativity, sacrifice, or gratitude—rather than always focusing on what you need or want.

Armed with information about yourself at your best, you can try to leverage those strengths with more purpose and consis-tency. You might even become aware of other good-attitude behaviors you could add to your repertoire.

work the plans, get it done, bank the successes, and try to get better at working together.

It's not personal. It's business.

CHAPTER SUMMARY

- Real influence is the holy grail of the go-to person.
    - Others want to work with them, do things for them, make good use of their time, and help them gain even more power.
- What makes the mathematics of real influence so peculiar is that it is not a zero-sum game:
    - Its value resides in the minds of others, but it works to your benefit.
    - It is completely intangible but can have enormous real-world consequences.
    - It can accrue quickly and grow quickly, but it is a long-term asset.
    - It's incredibly valuable, but you cannot buy it.
    - People will do things for you based on it, but there is no quid pro quo involved.
    - Spending it, lending it, and giving it away just makes its value grow.
    - It builds and builds whenever you add value for others.
- By relentlessly adding value in service to others, you systematically build value in the thoughts and feelings of others, thereby enriching yourself and everyone you deal with, which allows you to add even more value for others.

3

Lead from Wherever You Are

Up, Down, Sideways . . . and Diagonal

Nate works as a manufacturing manager in a major company that makes truck steering systems. To do his job, he regularly collaborates across the organization, whether it's with purchasing or quality or engineering. One of his biggest frustrations is when things don't go well with his counterpart from another department. It's never clear how to resolve the problem or who has the final word on a disagreement. "Whenever I ask my boss to intervene on my behalf, back me up, and help me get what I need," Nate says, "his first, second, and third response is almost always, 'Work things out at your own level.'"

That response has become one of the mantras of the collaboration revolution. "Work things out at your level" effectively pushes as much communication, decision making, and cooperative action as far down the chain of command as possible. When it works well, everything runs more smoothly and swiftly: information exchange, planning, resource sharing, and execution. It also reduces unnecessary problems and waste.

When people *don't* work things out at their own level and get in the habit of going over each other's heads, to the boss or the boss's boss, trust and confidence within work relationships suffer, along with the work itself. Getting things done indirectly through the boss is not the best way to make your expectations clear and make a solid plan. That diminution in planning leads to further delays, mistakes, and resentment.

So, what is Nate's gripe with "work it out at your own level"? "The problem," says Nate, "is I don't have *the authority* I need to work things out at my level. We don't always have the same agenda. We have competing priorities and limited resources, not to mention egos."

The Authority Conundrum

Nate is grappling with what I call "the authority conundrum." The goal is to empower collaboration throughout the organization as far down the chain of command as possible. But when there's a problem and you're left to work things out at your own level, by definition nobody has the power of rank to resolve things swiftly and efficiently. And the conundrum emerges even when you are dealing with people in diagonal roles—up or down. One person might have a higher rank, but no one has direct authority, which complicates the relationship even more.

So, to Nate's point, when you have conflicting agendas, priorities, resource needs, and egos, you get into power struggles. That's why so many people in Nate's position "escalate the matter," which is corporate-speak for going over each other's heads.

The fact is that despite the collaboration revolution, with its flatter organizations and self-managed project teams, there is always *somebody* in charge who is making decisions. Choices are considered up and down the chain of command. At your own level, there will always be conflicts that can't be worked out.

What can you do? There are three logical possibilities:

1. You can escalate conflicts and try to get your boss to intervene on your behalf, which might mean further escalation to your boss's boss—which may or may not produce a resolution.

2. You can resist escalations and remain frozen in conflicts at your own level.

3. You can try to collaborate as if you have all the authority you need—ignore the proper lines of authority, sidestep or end-run the chain of command, and assume or presume what the boss's answer would be to the problem.

"Proceed until apprehended. That was our strategy," says Chris, a former executive in a federal agency. She was describing how her team dealt with the many unclear lines of authority in its working relationships with people in other offices, agencies, and departments. "We'd get an interagency request, or we'd have some initiative we were keen to pursue that required participation by another office," she says. "Nobody had the authority. It was like the Wild West."

How did that work out? "Sometimes it was fine, if all the people involved were on the same page," says Chris. "But too often we were just moving ahead blindly until it would come back to bite us. We'd all buy in to somebody's great idea and invest time and energy and budget dollars. Then it would turn out there was no support at higher levels. So, the whole thing would get scratched. Or we'd decline a request, and then be overruled by the bosses and end up getting a late start. Or we'd disagree about something and fight it out until one or the other prevailed, or not."

Too many people find themselves, in effect, proceeding until apprehended, leading to the kinds of real business problems and costs that Chris describes. That's often the net effect of "work things out at your own level."

Meantime, most people in the workplace need a lot more guidance than they get when it comes to managing their sideways and diagonal working relationships. But they feel they are discouraged from going to their managers for that guidance until things are already going wrong. Or they sidestep authority and go in the wrong direction until it comes back to bite them.

The ad hoc, unstructured, as-needed communication typical of the collaboration revolution often breeds unnecessary problems that get out of control—leading to delays, errors, squandered resources, and plenty of relationship damage.

What's the go-to person to do?

Align, Align, Align

The answer is *alignment*. How you align yourself in terms of decision making and support—and with whom—is the first core mechanism of becoming indispensable at work.

"I don't have the power myself, so I go get the power from my boss," says Fernando, an IT service tech manager in a large accounting firm. "We have a system for ranking service tickets and project work, but of course every ticket is somebody's special urgent priority. Everybody wants their IT issues put higher in the queue. Before I took over the team, people here were in the habit of going over the tech manager's head or even going to the boss or the boss's boss. Nobody does that now."

What changed?

Fernando says, "Since I took over, we beat them to the punch every time. *We go over our own heads* before anyone else can. I've already gone to my boss, every time, before anybody else can go over my head. My techs have already come to me, every time, before anybody else. We are all totally aligned. So, there is no point to going over our heads."

Does that mean Fernando has to check with his boss every time he makes a move? And do his techs have to check with Fernando every time before they make a move? "Only if we don't already know the answer," says Fernando. "If we don't know, then we'd better check. But we almost always already know the answer. I don't speak for my boss, but I might as well, because nine times out of ten, I already know what he would say. The same is true with my techs. They already know what

I would say, in almost every case, so they might as well speak for me."

Can you say the same about you and your boss and your chain of command? Are you so aligned with your boss and your boss's boss that you might as well speak for them because you already know what they would say?

Remember, you are not in charge, but somebody is. Decisions are being made at a higher level. If you are going to have the power to operate without authority and work things out at your own level—what I call working sideways (and diagonal)—then, first, you've got to align yourself with the people making decisions: you've got to go vertical.

Go Vertical Before Going Sideways (or Diagonal)

Going vertical is one of the secrets to becoming an indispensable go-to person. At work you deal with so many people from all over the organization chart—up, down, sideways, and diagonal—that in order to keep your priorities straight and set yourself up for success, you must align yourself vertically along the way. You need to know clearly where you have discretion and where you don't. The only place to get that clarity is from above.

When you don't know an answer, you'd better check with your boss. Over time, you will get the answers to many questions that recur, and you'll learn more about the organization's overarching objectives and policies, ground rules, politics, and standing marching orders. The more you check, up front and in advance, before proceeding, the more situational awareness you'll gain—and the less likely you'll be apprehended going in the wrong direction.

The same goes for your direct reports. You must align with them so they understand their marching orders and have the authority to make choices and get their work done.

So, vertical alignment (up and down) is your anchor because:

- If nine times out of ten you already know exactly what your boss (and your boss's boss) would say, you have a lot more power to work sideways (and diagonal)—to communicate, decide, and take action—with confidence. That power comes from managing up.

- If nine times out of ten your direct reports already know exactly what you (and your boss) would say, then they have a lot more power, too. That's the power you give your direct reports by managing down—aka, just plain managing.

- It is also much easier to deal with sideways and diagonal colleagues who ensure their own vertical alignment, with their own bosses and direct reports. Otherwise you may think you are making decisions and taking action with colleagues at your own level only to find that they were never empowered to do business with you in the first place. While you *can't* control that, you *can* try to check up front.

What does it take to attain such vertical alignment? Let's start by looking at managing up (managing your bosses) *and* down (just plain managing your direct reports), because what needs to happen for alignment in both directions is the same: regular, structured communication at every step to clarify priorities, marching orders, and expectations, and to plan, track performance, and

Extreme Alignment

Thriving in the collaboration revolution means staying in alignment with your boss, your direct reports, and your colleagues (sideways and diagonal) in the organization. To make yourself truly indispensable, go the extra mile with extreme alignment:

- *Regularly provide drafts or samples of your work in progress.* Don't wait until a routine review of the work comes along; by then, you might discover you've been doing a task the wrong way for quite some time. Even if you have a clear deliverable with a concrete deadline, don't wait until you deliver the final product to find out if it meets the expectations. Instead, check in with your boss, direct report, or colleagues early on. That means not just describing but actually showing drafts or samples: "This is an example of the product I'm building. Does this meet your requirements? What adjustments should I make?"

- *Ask your boss, direct reports, or colleagues to watch you work.* Watching you complete a task will give them a clear view of what you are doing and how you are doing it. This also gives you an opportunity to have your work spot-checked to identify and solve any hidden problems. For example, if you manage a database, ask your collaborators to walk through some records, chosen at random, with you to check for quality. If you write reports, ask colleagues to look at early drafts or draft sections.

- *In every one-on-one conversation, provide a full and honest account of your activities.* Account for exactly what you've done on your assignments for that person since your last conversation: "These are the concrete actions I've taken. This is what I did and how I did it. These are the steps I followed in order to meet or exceed the expectations we set together." Once you've given an honest account, ask to clarify next steps. As long as you are engaged in an ongoing, consistent, one-on-one dialogue with that person, this element will become routine.

- *Use self-monitoring tools.* Track your concrete actions by making good, rigorous use of project plans, checklists, and activity logs. Monitor in writing whether you are meeting the goals and deadlines laid out in a project plan. Make notes and report to your collaborators at regular intervals. Use an activity log, a diary noting exactly what you are doing all day, including breaks and interruptions. Each time you move on to a new activity, note the time and the new activity. Even if you do this only periodically, you will still acquire valuable information about how efficiently you work, and you can make adjustments accordingly.

- *Spread the word.* Ask customers, vendors, coworkers, and everyone else you work with to give you honest feedback about your performance in relation to them. Ask them in writing, "How am I doing?" People talk. Word spreads. You should know what people think about your work. Use that data as feedback to help you improve.

solve problems while they are still small. If you are anybody's boss, that is a huge responsibility. Do not take it lightly. And if your boss is not managing you, then you had better start managing your boss. (See the sidebar "Extreme Alignment.")

Vertical Alignment: Managing Up—and Down

Before anything else, you need to go up the chain of command, on a regular basis, to ensure you have the power you need to do your job. Get in the habit of going over your own head at every step and align with your boss through regular structured dialogue.

Align with Your Boss to Manage Competing Priorities

Let's say you are a would-be go-to person who also assumes a role in a cross-functional working group or a special project team. At the outset, you might be asked to commit a percentage of your daily or weekly schedule, say, 20 percent, for some period of time, say, three months.

What happens? Soon that 20 percent turns into 30 percent or 50 percent, and three months turns into four or five or six. Often, this is because of "scope creep"—the bounds of the project expand. What happens to you, though, is what I call "role creep." Your role in this special project takes on its own life and starts to take over your job.

You try to deal with it. You work harder and have a good attitude. After all, you think, how long can this last? At project team meetings, you see you're not alone in being late on your deliverables. Everything is behind schedule, and it looks as if this project will continue even longer than you thought.

At this point, you have three options:

1. Try to be a superhero and keep doing everything. Perhaps you will be able to do it all forever. But you will probably find yourself becoming more and more overcommitted. Perhaps you succumb to siege mentality and start resisting every other opportunity that comes your way. Meanwhile, you risk errors and delays. Maybe you disappoint your boss or your project team. You probably end up disappointing both.

2. Double down on your commitment to your role in this project and diminish your commitment to your primary job.

3. Diminish your commitment to this project and double down on your commitment to your primary job.

Regardless of the option you choose, the most important thing is, first, go vertical and manage up. You need to be *in dialogue with your boss* on the matter, checking in every step of the way.

Aisha is a marketing executive who found herself overcommitted after being pulled into a seemingly endless project on a cross-functional team. She wisely sat down with her boss to discuss what to do. It turned out that neither saw much of a choice; the project had to be done and so did her regular job. Aisha was the only real candidate for both. But she felt a whole lot better making the choice to play the superhero *with* her boss's support. Now they both shared responsibility for the fact that Aisha was carrying an overwhelming workload for an extended period of time.

Aisha kept up the regular structured dialogue with her boss, and at some point, the boss saw that she was doing a spectacular job balancing the overload—and he recommended her for a promotion. But even if Aisha had begun to drown in overcommitment and not handled it well, because she and her boss stayed in dialogue, they were both more likely to have seen that coming. Her boss could have provided her with extra support, perhaps someone who could backfill part of Aisha's work in her primary job or on the extra project, or both.

Likewise, if Aisha and her boss had chosen option two, to double down on the cross-functional project, Aisha would still maintain close contact with her boss to help find and support someone to backfill her work in her primary job. She'd need to document her current best practices in the form of step-by-step work instructions for all her transferable primary tasks, responsibilities, and projects (if she hadn't already prepared these job aids for herself, being the go-to person that she is). She would likely assist in training the person backfilling her role.

Because she made these moves in alignment with her boss, everything would probably go more smoothly than if she were just winging it on her own. In the process, she would have the opportunity to help build up a new go-to person to fill in at her primary job. That would enhance her leadership skills and experience, as well as her growing network of go-to people.

Finally, what if Aisha had chosen option three instead, telling her boss that she really didn't like being on the project team and wanted to be able to commit at least 80 percent of her time to her primary job? Or maybe her boss has really missed Aisha and wants her back full-time. Either way, there would be some political work to be done with the project team members and the executive sponsor of the cross-functional team. Aisha's boss might or might not get involved to help her diminish her role in—or remove her altogether from—the project.

But by staying in close consultation and cooperation with her boss as well as with her collaborators on the cross-functional team, Aisha would be much more likely to win the support she needs. Again, her withdrawal from the project fully or partially might present another great opportunity for Aisha to help develop somebody else to take over some or all of her role on the project, lifting them up as a new go-to person and expanding her network.

Align with Your Direct Reports

Just as you must stay aligned with your boss, your direct reports need to stay aligned with you, and you need to take responsibility for ensuring that alignment. Your direct reports don't want to waste time and energy going in the wrong direction any more than you do. They need your guidance, direction, support, and coaching to set them up for success in their work and help them get their needs met. Being in charge of other people is a huge responsibility. Don't take it lightly.

Practicing regular, structured dialogue with every single person who reports to you is how you make sure they have the power they need to work things out at their level—to make decisions and take action. Are there problems that need solving now or that are hovering on the horizon? Are there any needed extra resources you should secure, or any instructions or goals that aren't clear? Has anything happened since the last time you talked to the person that you should know about?

Just like Aisha, and just like you, your direct reports probably have too much to do and not enough time. In addition to their primary job, in which they report to you, they are also likely being drawn into other projects—sideways and diagonal.

So, first, closely track your direct reports' workloads—monitor every individual's available productive capacity (what many refer to as "bandwidth"—in other words, "Exactly how much more work can you handle?").

Second, make sure *you* are not the one who is overcommitting your own direct reports. So often, managers end up making commitments to their own boss, or to their sideways or diagonal colleagues, that have huge implications for their subordinates, leaving them to scramble in order to accomplish everything.

Third, when your direct reports do start taking on so much that they risk overcommitment, use your regular structured dialogues with them to help them balance all of their competing priorities by providing the kind of ongoing support Aisha's boss gave her. (See the sidebar "Helpers, Experts, and Rogues.")

That's exactly the kind of boss Joel tries to be. Joel, a research manager in a biotech firm, often finds his team members in demand for side projects because of their expertise. Those are the employees to whom he pays the most special attention. He stays in especially close contact with them and helps them watch out for project scope creep and role creep. He regularly asks them how they are allocating their time between their regular tasks and responsibilities and their competing priorities on whatever projects they're pulled into.

Joel also regularly talks through two key questions with those direct reports: What might not get done? What might be delayed? If the balance starts to become untenable, Joel helps those employees make choices—and sometimes he offers to intervene by talking with the leader of the outside team. But usually he's able to help his direct reports eliminate or delay some less critical tasks, or develop backup plans, if needed, to provide additional support. That includes helping them find and develop backfill personnel to relieve some of their workload.

This is yet another illustration of the incredible value of continually developing your network of go-to people. When one of your direct reports is truly overcommitted, you may not always be able to redistribute work to another member of your immediate team. They might be verging on overcommitment themselves. But it just might be an opportunity to add a new go-to person to your team. Maybe there is a sideways or diagonal colleague who has worked with you or your direct reports, and they've already proven themselves. If you've also proven yourself to them, maybe that colleague will want to join your team.

Be careful about poaching talent from other managers, but always be on the lookout to identify new talent (including internally) and be prepared to train them to bolster the team. All at once you can increase the head count on your team, provide support and relief for your overloaded direct reports, and have the opportunity to build up a new go-to person.

When You Are the Customer at Someone Else's Mercy

At some point, you or your subordinates will likely find you are at the mercy of someone on whom you—or your subordinates— must rely, but who has no real stake in your (or their) success or

Helpers, Experts, and Rogues

Certain types of employees, more so than others, tend to jump into projects outside their normal jobs. I call these people "helpers, experts, and rogues."

Helpers get pulled away from their regular work because they are genuinely open and tend to be good at solving problems—and they have a hard time saying no. So people are always asking them for help.

Experts are always getting asked to field a question or take a look at something because they usually know the answers.

Rogues are drawn away from their work because they become intrigued by some interesting idea or initiative, often their own, but also from some other rogue.

Helpers, experts, and rogues continually find themselves explaining to their bosses why their regular work is falling behind. And it's usually because they were busy doing something that really should have taken a backseat to their regular work.

If you're a boss to one of these types, you might be tempted to say, "Stop doing all that other work and do your job!" But at the same time, you know that being a helper, expert, or rogue can be a positive thing. Those people end up doing some pretty interesting stuff—often the very things that make them go-to people for some of your best customers.

So instead of just shutting them down, you can assist the helper, expert, or rogue to *own* what they do. Make their particular tendency part of your ongoing dialogue with them. Stay aligned with them at every step of their workload and how they are managing their competing priorities. You can help them by setting clear ground rules for how to make time for their side work—without getting distracted from their primary responsibilities.

For example, discuss how much time—as their boss—you are comfortable with them using their skills as helpers, experts, or rogues. What criteria could help them decide whether an outside project is something they should do or not? Are there certain people you want them to avoid, or others they should go out of their way to serve?

With a time budget and clear guidelines, you can help these people document all their extra work in a time log. Then you can give them proper credit, or if the work they're doing turns out to be of no value from your perspective, you can shut it down.

What if you realize you are a helper, expert, or rogue? Again, it's best to own it instead of risking having your side operations continually shut down. Use your ongoing dialogue with your boss to get help with addressing your tendency, as outlined earlier. If it turns out that your boss deems the extra work you do of no value to the organization, then you'll need to seriously consider what that means for you. If you're convinced your boss is wrong, be prepared to make a business case for what you do.

whom you (or they) can't hold accountable, or both. Whether it's a counterpart in another department you must cooperate with to accomplish a task, or some outsider who holds the purse strings on a pet project, you as a boss will need to help your subordinate manage that tricky relationship. And if you're the subordinate, you'll need to ask your boss for the help and backup you need.

When you are at someone else's mercy, you are essentially the customer, requiring help or cooperation from someone sideways or diagonal in the organization. Again, vertical alignment is critical—upward with your boss for guidance and support, or downward with your direct report who needs your help. And that alignment should happen sooner rather than later.

Shantel, a gifted graphic designer at a global consulting firm, provides a cautionary tale. It was the end of her workday, and once again she was sitting at her computer, awaiting text for a four-color brochure that was due to her boss in the morning. The copywriter, who was based in another time zone, had promised it to her hours ago.

Shantel already had done everything she could with the design, having only the brochure title and company logo to work with. Now it was 5 p.m. and the copywriter still hadn't delivered the text. Shantel wanted to give the writer the benefit of the doubt. Something else might have come up.

But Shantel had been down this road before. In the past, this writer had made similar promises but failed to deliver his copy until late in *his* day—which was more like 8 p.m. Shantel's time. He was on track to do it again, meaning that, even if Shantel were to badger the writer again now, in the best case Shantel would be sitting at her computer until at least 10 p.m., working his brochure text into her design for the morning deadline.

Don't allow yourself to get into this situation over and over again, like Shantel. Do not wait until your work is due and either sacrifice your evening or end up trying to explain to your boss that you missed a deadline because your colleague didn't come through on time.

Instead, keep your boss regularly apprised—well ahead of a deadline—about problems you foresee regarding someone who needs to provide a key piece of a project. You are not asking your boss to intervene or go to the other person's boss. You are alerting your boss and asking for support, such as:

- More flexibility on the deadline in question

- Advice on further steps you might take to get what you need from your colleague

- Recommendations for alternative talent you could work with to get what you need to stay on track, if there's no wiggle room on the deadline

In your ongoing dialogue with your boss, think ahead and think aloud—together—through the resources you need to do your job (especially when they involve the cooperation of sideways colleagues), at every step. Articulate exactly what you are going to need, from whom, when, and how you are planning to get it. Ask for advice about how to get what you need on schedule. Maybe there are tips the boss can share about getting certain things from certain people or teams or departments.

Then keep your boss updated, early and often, if you're running into obstacles or delays. Talk through backup plans, workarounds, and what to do if you just cannot get what's required.

Alignment Also Means Gathering and Sharing Intel

Knowledge is power.

Keep your eyes and ears open for valuable intelligence up and down the chain of command. That doesn't mean listening to and spreading gossip. It means learning from your direct reports about what's happening on the front lines, from your boss about what's occurring in the executive boardroom, and from everyone else about anything in between.

It's not enough to align yourself, after the fact, with decisions and priorities up and down. You want to help inform those decisions and priorities, and you want to understand as much as you can. In a world of infinite business data, human intelligence—what people are thinking and saying—is still incredibly valuable. Often that intelligence is there but is not communicated up and down the chain of command. So when you gather and share intel, you are telling your boss that you care about how your job fits into the organization, and you are showing your direct reports that you care about their experience and perspective and value what they are learning.

Here's how to do it:

- Ask your boss for regular updates about key decisions made at a higher level, especially changes in high-level priorities, personnel, policies, procedures, systems, or resource allocations.

- Make sure you understand how any changes might affect your planning or that of your direct reports. Clarify what information is meant to be kept confidential, at least for now, and what information and messages you should communicate systematically down the chain of command to your peers and direct reports.

- At the same time, keep your boss informed of any important developments or reportable facts you observe at your level or learn from your peers or direct reports. That will help your boss see around the corner to any upcoming risks, challenges, needs, or opportunities you perceive on the front lines.

- Keep your boss apprised of what's going on in your other dialogues with your own subordinates and other colleagues: Are you dealing with or anticipating any personnel issues? Performance problems? Conflict on the team? Superstars who may need special rewards? Staffing-level changes? Training needs? Other resource issues?

- And if you are someone's boss, make sure you are driving the same kind of intelligence gathering and sharing conversations with your direct reports.

Aligning Yourself Sideways—and Diagonal

If you are doing the work I've just described to align vertically, up and down, at every step, then you'll be in a much stronger position to maintain alignment in your sideways and diagonal working relationships too. If you have structured communication in those sideways and diagonal relationships, it likely occurs in the form of regular project team meetings. But a lot of critical communication will also happen in informal side conversations that are highly unstructured: ad hoc hallway encounters, lunch, quick text updates, phone calls, and office drop-ins, not to mention cross-talk and side conversations in those otherwise structured project team meetings.

Formal Structured Meetings

Meetings can be great opportunities, but not all meetings are great. There are really only three good reasons for a meeting:

1. To create a feeling of belonging and togetherness

2. To communicate a bunch of information to a bunch of people in the same way at the same time

3. To brainstorm about a project or deal with an open question, such as planning interdependent project handoffs in which multiple people need to hear and respond to each other

With so much interdependent work going on and handoffs to plan, meetings have become ubiquitous in the collaboration revolution workplace. People often tell me that they have no time to work because they spend their whole workday in meetings on top of meetings, and too often, the meetings are not so great. The stakes are high because every single minute consumed in any meeting is multiplied by the number of people. A thirty-minute meeting with eight people consumes four hours of productive capacity (time in which people could be working on something else).

I'll never forget the first time I walked into a corporate conference room that had a posted placard outlining rules of conduct for meetings. The list included gems ranging from "If you are the host, distribute an agenda in advance to all participants" to "Silence your phones" to "Please clean up after yourself." I asked the person sitting next to me, "Gee, is that really necessary?" She said, "Yeah, people are irritated by the sign. It's sort of infantilizing. But actually, some people are just horrible in meetings."

Since then, I cannot count the number of conference rooms in which someone, officially or not, has posted a placard with similar kinds of meeting rules. Nonetheless, people still hold meetings without clear agendas or, despite a clear agenda, they don't follow it. Or they go way over the allotted time, digress, hold one-on-one cross-talk conversations on the side, or try to multitask with handheld devices or laptops (sometimes pretending to take notes) and then chime in with a point that's already been made. Or they come late, leave early, make noise, eat smelly food—you name it.

Just as people notice when colleagues are especially horrible at running or attending meetings, they also notice people who are great at meetings. Be that person.

First, be known as a great meeting citizen. That means, be informed and be reliable. Make sure you don't double- or triple-book yourself for meetings. It's amazing how common this has become among would-be go-to people because they think it makes them seem busy. Being double-booked is not impressive. You cannot be in more than one place at a time, and it's distracting if you're hopping in and out of meetings in progress. If you have conflicts, make a choice and choose the most important meeting, not the easiest one. That doesn't mean the meeting with the most big shots or the highest-profile work, but rather the meeting where you play an important role and have the most value to add. If you are not sure, align with your boss.

Then, before attending any meeting or presentation, make sure you know what the meeting is about and whether your attendance is required or requested. One of the biggest favors you can do for yourself is becoming savvy about which meetings to attend and which ones not to. Again, make sure to align with your boss. The key is knowing exactly what your role in the meeting is: What information are you responsible for communicating or gathering? Prepare in advance any material you should review or read before the meeting. Are there any conversations you need to have before the meeting? If you are making a presentation, of course you'll prepare even more. Ask yourself exactly what value you have to offer the group and then be sure you deliver that value.

If you are not a primary actor, or you don't have some other clear role in the meeting, try not to say a single word that will unnecessarily lengthen it. And practice good meeting manners: Do not try to multitask or make unnecessary noise or activity. Stay focused on the business at hand. Listen carefully and learn. If you are tempted to speak up, ask yourself: Is this a point that everyone needs to hear, right here and now? If you have a question, consider whether the question is important to the purpose of the meeting or whether you could get your question answered later by referring to a document or asking someone.

Informal Unstructured Communication

What about communication that takes place *outside* the formal meeting? Those tidbits someone drops on you at the coffee station or that text or quick check-in from a colleague can be every bit as important as the formal information and discussion you get when sitting in meetings.

The trick is to put some structure in those informal exchanges. Just as you would note and apply what you learn during a formal meeting, you should capture and leverage as much informal information as possible. In fact, informal communication can be the ultimate tool when you're asked to "work it out at your own level."

So, pay close attention to all those unstructured interactions that come your way between or before or right after a meeting, or even side (or cross) talk during meetings. Those seemingly one-off communications, if they involve any substantive talk about the work, can be key. There is often critical information in the cross talk at a meeting or a quick postmeeting huddle. The same goes for all those emails, texts, quick calls, hallway chats, and drop-bys.

Don't let it stay in the ether. Put as much structure as you possibly can in those unstructured informal communications:

- Stop the person who is delivering the aside

- Visibly take notes

- Then follow up in writing to confirm the communication and try to schedule a structured follow-up one-on-one conversation

Bud, a grain buyer working in a billion-dollar agricultural co-op, sent me an email recently to tell me how well this simple tactic has worked for him since he started using it after one of my seminars. Bud is always on the road helping farmers sell their grain. His work involves navigating transactions with numerous collaboration partners—contractors, schedulers, truckers, grain elevator operators, processors, financers, and sometimes more.

Bud wrote in an email, "I just took it for granted that most of my communication with most of these people was so informal and unstructured. After the program, I started carrying a notebook. I pull out my notebook and take notes at each stop, all day. My end-of-the-day routine now is to send out a bunch of emails based on my notes. It just squares up what I did during the day and keeps things from slipping through the cracks." My favorite part of Bud's email came near the end: "One of the producers said to me, last time I was there, 'Heck. You're writing everything down now, I notice. You must be getting serious about this business.' I told him, 'Yes sir. You bet I'm serious.'"

Add structure to unstructured interactions, and you will get much better substance. That is especially true when it comes to interruptions—those inconvenient questions or comments that someone drops on you when you're right in the middle of something else.

How to deal with interruptions. Who are your regular interrupters? And whom do you find yourself interrupting on a regular basis? Often, seemingly one-off communications can become an important, ongoing conversation. Again, the key is to add structure to those interruptions.

Try it. When one of your regular interrupters next interrupts you, don't dismiss the conversation, but after absorbing the interruption, suggest scheduling a one-on-one meeting. In between now and your scheduled one-on-one, suggest that you each keep a list of what you want to discuss with the other—and that you each prepare a bit before you meet.

Imagine how much more productive that conversation is likely to be than all those interruptions. If it goes really well, maybe, at the end, schedule another conversation. Maybe you will get into a cadence of regular, structured communication, instead of all those unstructured interruptions.

This works especially well with high-maintenance customers and clients who think nothing of interrupting you because they are the ones paying the company all that money. They are often your top priority, so you know you'd better welcome and even embrace their interruptions. But you can serve them a whole lot better, and save yourself a lot of aggravation, by paying attention to the frequency of their interruptions and scheduling a regular one-on-one to get ahead of them. If you build the right cadence of structured one-on-ones, you will obviate most interruptions, with the exception of real emergencies.

What if you're the person who regularly interrupts others? Maybe you think nothing of peppering your own vendors or direct reports with questions or comments while they're trying to work. Or maybe you find yourself interrupting your boss or that special go-to colleague almost daily because you need guidance or help.

Try, instead, asking those people for one-on-one meetings. It can be lunch or coffee or a fifteen-minute conversation in the conference room. Save up your questions and prepare for the meeting in advance. Your direct reports, vendors, boss, or colleagues will thank you. Nobody's at their best when they are being interrupted. Why would you want to be anybody's regular interrupter?

Diagonal Relationships Can Be Especially Tricky

What about diagonal relationships—the ones where you're working with people above or below your position on the organization chart, but with whom you don't have a direct reporting relationship?

They might be someone higher up, maybe a peer of your boss or even your boss's boss, but with whom you are sharing a task, responsibility, or project. Or you may find yourself working with someone who doesn't report to you but reports to one of your lateral colleagues, another manager at your level or below but not in your immediate chain of command.

What's tricky about these relationships is the power differential. But it's indirect power, which can lead to misunderstandings and stepped-on toes. When you are managing diagonally down, make sure to stay aligned with that person's direct boss. If anything changes in your working relationship with this individual, keep the boss in the loop.

When you are managing diagonally up, make sure to stay aligned with your boss. You don't want to disappoint this other senior person, but make sure you keep your boss's authority in the situation front and center—and treat your boss with the utmost respect. Do this even if you are actually in "manager shopping" mode and looking to make a move. Even if you are consciously auditioning to possibly switch to this other manager, show that new manager how you operate. Demonstrate your respect for authority, structured communication, and alignment at every step. It's the right thing to do and the impression you always want to make.

Lead from Wherever You Are: Up, Down, Sideways, and Diagonal

The collaboration revolution has ushered in a huge increase in interdependent working relationships where lines of authority are not clear, along with the rise of so-called self-managed teams and the thinning out of management ranks in many organizations, all of which flatten hierarchies and widen the spans of control for managers. In this environment, the only way to make sure you are aligned and going in the right direction is to lead up, down, sideways, and diagonally—from wherever you are right now. What does that look like?

When explaining leadership, General Schwarzkopf often cited an old military cliché: "When in command, take charge." Let me amend that for the collaboration revolution workplace: *Whether or not you are in command, take charge.*

One of Schwarzkopf's colleagues, another four-star US Army general, who must remain anonymous, once told me, "There is only one tool for leading others: communication." Then he said, "It's amazing how many people want to be leaders, but there is no rhyme or reason to how they communicate." Let me put a fine point on that: *If you want to take charge of anyone anytime, you must communicate with rhyme and reason.*

My firm's decades of research show that the more rhyme and reason—substance and structure—that you put into your communication in any working relationship, the better things will go: fewer unnecessary problems occur, and those that are identified are solved more quickly; resources are better planned and less often squandered; people are more likely to concur about what they've agreed on; and fewer conflicts occur within the ranks.

That's true whether you are leading (i.e., communicating with) people up, down, sideways, diagonal or—like most people in the workplace—in all four directions. Just remember, the order of operations is very important: start by aligning yourself vertically, with your boss and the chain of command by managing up, and down with your direct reports. That's your anchor. Then you can go sideways—and diagonal.

Sideways and diagonal are always the directions where the lines of authority are least clear. So, you and your colleagues need to "work things out at your own level." Most often that means making really good choices about when to say no and how to say yes. "Yes" is where all the action is, so you'd better not waste your yeses by overpromising or failing to plan.

CHAPTER SUMMARY

- Align by going vertical before going sideways (or diagonal).

- Align up by going over your own head to your boss, at every step, through regular structured dialogue.

- Align down through structured dialogue with your direct reports so they understand their marching orders and have the authority to make the necessary choices to get their work done.

- Once you are anchored up and down, you can go sideways—and diagonal.

- Be known as a great meeting citizen.

- Put structure and substance into more of your unstructured communication.

- Schedule regular one-on-ones with your regular interrupters and with those whom you interrupt on a regular basis.

- When you are managing diagonally down, stay aligned with that person's direct boss. When you are managing diagonally up, stay aligned with your boss.

- Lead from wherever you are: up, down, sideways and diagonal.

- Whether or not you are in command, take charge. If you want to take charge of anyone anytime, you must communicate with rhyme and reason.

4

When to Say No and How to Say Yes

All day long, the asks keep coming at you from every direction—from your boss, your direct reports, from your sideways and diagonal colleagues. They come from out of the blue from somebody you've never even heard of. Or from across the table in the middle of a meeting. Maybe they come by email, even in the middle of an endless reply-all email thread. Or in a text or instant message. Or someone pokes their head into your workspace.

For every ask, the answer, at the core, is either yes or no. Often, the answer—yes or no—is simply not within your discretion to make. The decision has already been made—implicitly or explicitly—by your boss or someone further up the chain of command. That's why most of the previous chapter deals with maintaining vertical alignment with your boss. You need to know with clarity all of the decisions that you don't need to make because they have already been made. Your direct reports need the same clarity from you.

Knowing what decisions are not for you to make is like having guardrails. Guardrails can be very empowering. Once you really understand the constraints, what is not within your discretion, it becomes clear what is: everything else. And that's a lot.

Within those guardrails of vertical alignment is where you have the discretion—the authority and the burden—to field those asks all day long and make tough decisions about yes and no.

The Incredible Power of Reimagining Yes and No

Decisions about yes and no are all about opportunity cost:

- Every bad no is a missed opportunity or a delayed (and maybe soured) opportunity if the no gets overturned

- Every bad yes is a waste of time, energy, and money that will crowd out a better opportunity

- Every good no—or not yet—makes room for a better opportunity

- Every good yes is a chance to make the most of a good opportunity and serve others by adding value and building your real influence

When you make bad decisions about yes and no, you have worse opportunities and experiences today and have less discretion tomorrow. You don't get to add as much value or develop as many positive relationships.

When you make good decisions, you have better opportunities, better chances to add value and build positive relationships, and earn more discretion for tomorrow.

The stakes are high.

Some people have a strong bias for no. *No* seems strong because it shuts down activity and it seems less risky because it's much harder to prove out, good or bad. But if all you've got to show for your decisions is a pile of noes, where's the value?

Yes has a reputation for being the less powerful word: the term "yes man" is pejorative, meant to connote somebody who just goes along. But yes is where all the action is. When your yeses go right, that's when you hit the jackpot: serving others, adding value, collaborating successfully, and growing your real influence. Yes is the beginning of a collaboration, the start of something. Yes is full of potential, upward-spiraling power.

Every decision about yes and no really comes down to how you're going to spend your time.

How Will You Spend Your Time?

Start by understanding the hard truth that *you can't do everything*. Yes, you're getting bombarded by people who think that you *can* do everything. You simply must make choices among those competing priorities, agendas, and egos. Some things are not going to get done until later, and some things might not get done at all. That fact is inevitable.

Unless you accept the reality of competing priorities and make those tough choices better and sooner, at every step, you'll fall into overcommitment syndrome. But really, so much overcommitment syndrome comes from *wrong commitment* syndrome— aka, bad decisions about yes and no. That's how you end up with a lot of forced noes. If you don't make those choices sooner and better, someone else will, probably later and worse. Later, the best choices may no longer be available. You have to make choices. Make them good ones.

Why do we fail to do that time and again?

When Good People Make Bad Decisions

Some people simply say yes to everything, because they're trying to be good team players. Or they think "yes, yes, yes" is what will make them a go-to person.

Some people aren't even aware that they *are* making decisions, sometimes important decisions. Usually they've made the decisions by default, by not making a decision. That lack of awareness is usually how you get to the end of a long day wondering: "What did I even accomplish today?!" Upon reflection, you think of a bunch of decisions you made throughout the day that you didn't realize you'd made, or that you know you could have made better.

Sometimes the decisions are big ones that you might have to unmake tomorrow, but often they are micro-decisions in response to asks sprinkled among all the interactions occurring constantly at work between coworkers: "Could you help me with this?" "Do you have that piece of information?" "Resource?"

"Opinion?" Often these questions boil down to: "Will you please do your part so that I can do my part?"

Why are so many day-to-day yeses and noes so sloppy? The number one reason is that most people aren't very good at asking. They're not good at framing, explaining, spelling it out, or breaking it down. Sometimes they think they've made an ask, and you didn't even recognize it.

What about you? Maybe you, too, aren't so good at asking. You need things from your boss, cross-functional counterparts, and individuals on your project teams. Once in a while, you even need something from someone out of the blue. Maybe the ask, whether you are asking or being asked, seems relatively minor in the moment. So, when you give—or get—an inadvertent answer, it seems relatively inconsequential. But the sloppy ask so often leads to the sloppy yes or the sloppy no:

- You say yes to what looks like a one-off task: proofing a colleague's report on your joint project. But it actually needs a full rewrite and ends up becoming all-consuming. Or you say no to proofing the report and miss out on a chance to improve how your boss views the project, because the report is such a mess.

- You say no to lubricating the machine, but then the machine breaks and you can't get your work done. Or you say yes to lubricating the machine and discover, in the process, that the machine needs a lot more than just grease and fixing it is going to take all day.

- You say yes to helping interview new job candidates and then find out this requires traveling someplace distant and

The Key to Making Good Decisions

Think of the most basic decision-making tool, the weighing of pros and cons. The pros and cons list is just a set of predictions of likely outcomes to a particular choice.

Good decision making is mostly about being able to predict the likely outcomes—to see cause and effect—of one set of decisions and actions as opposed to another.

But experience alone does not teach good decision making. The key to learning from experience is paying close attention and aggressively drawing lessons: What causes led to what effects? What decisions or actions led to the current situation? If you can begin to see the patterns in causes and their effects, then you can start to think ahead with insight.

Have you ever played chess or another game of strategy? The key to success in games of strategy is thinking ahead.

inconvenient. Or you say no and discover the interviews will be with a group of candidates who might provide a great new perspective or with candidates who might be great to know going forward. Or you learn that the venue is a beautiful resort in the south of France that might be a fun place to bring your significant other for a tag-on holiday.

You cannot afford sloppy decision making about how you are going to spend your time at work. (See the sidebar "The Key to Making Good Decisions.")

Before making a move, you play out in your head the likely outcomes, often over a long sequence of moves and counter-moves. If I do A, the other player would probably respond with B. Then I would do C, and he would probably respond with D. Then I would do E, and he would probably respond with F. And so on. This is what strategic planners call a decision/action tree, because each decision or action is the beginning of a branch of responses and counter-responses. Each decision or action creates a series of possible responses, and each possible response creates a series of possible counter-responses.

Be aware of the decisions you are making all day long. Stop and reflect: think ahead about causes and effects, the decision/action tree.

Good Decision Making Requires Due Diligence

Sam is good at deciding. He tunes in to every ask, respects people's needs, and takes them very seriously. He rigorously considers his response, whether yes or no, because there is nothing like the gift of a good no. Often instead of no, he says, "Not yet," and sends people back to fine-tune their ask. Or he waits until he's tackled other priorities before he gives an answer. Then, when it is time for the yes, Sam sets up every yes for success with a clear plan of action including the sequence, timing, and ownership of all the next steps.

If you ask Sam his secret, he'll tell you he treats every decision as if it's an important investment decision—because it is. It's a decision about how he'll invest some amount of his limited time and energy.

You should do the same: treat every decision about yes and no as a choice about investing your time and energy. If you were making an investment decision in a responsible manner, you would follow a due diligence process. Due diligence is simply a careful investigation of any potential investment to confirm all the relevant facts and seek sufficient information to make an informed judgment so as to prevent unnecessary harm to either party in a transaction. The process protects both the asker and the party saying yes or no.

Take every request seriously enough to do your due diligence. Every good choice you make now will save you and everybody else so much time and trouble later. And it will also make others much more confident in your choices in the future.

Due diligence starts with insisting on a well-defined ask.

If you're the person asking, make sure you include enough information so the decision maker can make a better choice. And be prepared to answer more questions about your ask.

If you're the person being asked, do the following: (1) start by tuning in to the ask and the person making the request and asking good questions early and often at every step; (2) know when to say no and not yet; and (3) remember that yes is where all the action is.

What happens is usually something far from that ideal.

A Problem of Process

Consider the following case. One Monday morning, the president of the Americas region of a worldwide consumer-electronics company briefed his executive team on the marching orders he'd just received from the global CEO: develop a new blockbuster product that will be ready to launch the following year. This surprised no one. It was similar to the marching orders from the prior year.

The challenge really spoke to the entrepreneurial spirit in Res, who'd joined the company when it had acquired his invention and his small team, about two years earlier. Technically innovative as well as entrepreneurial, Res was now managing a research and development team. He was eager to make his mark again, this time with an idea for a new kind of machine—small, light, easy to transport, and easy to operate.

Res brought his preliminary drawings and the core elements of a working prototype to the cross-functional new-product innovation team that was choosing which products to move forward into development this year. He wanted the team to put a big bet behind his idea as the potential blockbuster product.

Salina, director of sales, was the first to speak up after Res's presentation. "Yes, yes, yes!" she said. "Think of all the market share we can take. What an opportunity!"

"No, no, no," countered Etan, the rather cautious director of quality and regulatory affairs. "This could be a risky endeavor."

"And," added Lira, the accountant, "it looks to be a very costly initial investment." Those were just a handful of the voices at the table. Everyone seemed to have a strong and very swift opinion: yes, yes, yes! or no, no, no! Yet, from the outside looking in, something wasn't quite right. There was something very wrong indeed: there was a very big question hiding in plain sight.

What Was the Ask?

No one really knew exactly what the ask was. At the simplest level, the CEO's marching order to the Americas' executive team was a giant ask, totally vague, and with everything at stake. The CEO could have specified which consumer segment to target, whether to go for a high average sale price versus high-volume product, whether to go after an existing product market with improvements to meet customer demand versus opening up a whole new market with something altogether novel, and on and on. The CEO was adamant, however, that each regional executive team should make such decisions for its own region, partly to leverage regional market savvy, but mostly to drive competition among the regions and generate more innovation bets overall for the company.

The regional president's ask to the executive team was equally vague: let's hand this off to the product innovation team. On the surface, this makes sense. Presidents have to trust their people to do their thing. But that's also how this decision became a research-led initiative because Res was the loudest, most confident voice at the table.

Res was eager to deliver the blockbuster product being asked for, and he had a passion project in his back pocket. He had been working on that lightweight machine for a long time. The problem was that he was presenting his dream for the product—he was preaching and selling—rather than spelling out a clear picture of the ask to the rest of the product innovation team: he wasn't realistically detailing the time commitments and other resources that would be required of each of the teams represented at the table.

Res's main point was simply, "We can do this!" But that was actually still an open question. All the teams represented at the table needed to assess how much time was required to develop this product in the next year, and which of their other responsibilities and projects they might have to postpone or cancel.

Res's second point was, "We don't have anything else that is nearly as promising and ready to go from research to development." That, too, was an open question. Other research engineers really should have been included in the discussion. After all, Res's proposal is not really "Let's pursue this!" but rather, "Let's pursue this instead of pursuing someone else's idea." To clarify the ask, the other ideas would need better consideration.

Res's third point was, "This is going to be huge!" He should have been asking, first, for sales, marketing, and accounting to help figure out the upside potential of this idea. Then he should have talked with engineering, quality, manufacturing, shipping, service, and accounting to figure out the investment costs of development and then the ongoing expense of cost of goods sold, so they could figure out potential profitability.

Everyone at the table, however, was focused on the vague marching orders from the top and on the promises Res offered. While there was plenty of pushback, the enthusiasm and volume of the yeses outweighed the caution of the noes.

What resulted was a green light for the next stage: "Let's start working on Res's idea and see where it goes."

Without sufficient rigor in the ask up front, the result was a yes without a plan. That green light, in turn, triggered a cascading series of further asks and answers, each consuming a considerable investment of time, energy, and money. Each of those further asks, it seemed, were all preordained, the yes already implied by the initial decision to green-light the next stage of development.

No one was considering other competing ideas from research because they were being crowded out by attention to Res's project. Anyway, the research engineers were drawn away from competing ideas and into discussions with the development engineers, who were trying to turn the prototype into a workable design: that also meant pulling in production managers, buyers from purchasing, and design quality-assurance specialists.

Meanwhile, marketing and sales were looking for ways to position, promote, and sell this new product. Accounting was involved in development budgeting as well as projecting possible revenues and profits. Service was anticipating warranty issues and replace-and-repair details. And on and on.

Each successive meeting of the cross-functional product innovation team became a rubber stamp for the next stage of Res's pet project. The ball was rolling now. There was plenty of new information coming into the picture, at every step. That meant plenty of wild goose chases, changes in direction, and rework. There were unexpected delays. Shifting budgets and schedules. But, after so much time, energy, and money had already been invested, stopping the project no longer seemed like a realistic option.

Issues were uncovered and resolved and details were fine-tuned, so costs went up and delays ensued at each step of the production path. Meantime, this cross-functional group met every other week to monitor, measure, and document progress; troubleshoot, problem solve, adjust—all with the goal of shepherding the product to the launch.

By the time it finally launched, the product was two years late and no longer the new and improved machine that had been promised. It was too heavy and far more costly to the company, once it factored in the massive warranty and service (including shipping) costs with all the returns and repairs in its two-year life span before it was withdrawn from the marketplace, never to be heard from again.

The team members, when last seen, were all still blaming each other, pointing fingers, especially at their cross-functional partners in other departments. But, in reality, the product's failure started at the very beginning with the sloppy asks from the CEO and the regional president, which produced the original sloppy yes from Res, followed by many more sloppy asks, sloppy yeses, and ultimately, under siege, some sloppy noes late in the game (remember, the key to a good no is *when*, i.e., coming at the right time).

By neglecting to clarify and interrogate the asks at the outset, the team made a catastrophically sloppy yes at the outset in an astoundingly casual manner, despite its formalized structure, setting in motion a cascade of sloppy decision making along the way, also despite the formalized structure of ongoing status meetings among the project team.

The Human Factor

What's going on here? Why didn't these highly trained professionals interrogate the ask—for the decisions enormous and small related to this project? Blame the "human factor." Simply said, decision making always involves people. This team comprised—as most teams do—very different kinds of people with a wide range of priorities, agendas, personalities, and egos. No matter how much decision and process may be shrouded in the data and logic, facts and reason, don't be fooled: there is always the human factor. In this case study, all the yes/no viewpoints and behavior sprang from those individual personalities and priorities.

Res is an entrepreneur and an inventor; his success is measured on the basis of how much his research team successfully develops and introduces new products. Res is also an enthusiast who likes to please.

Salina from sales just wants something the company believes its customers will want to buy, buy, buy. After all, they are measured based on sales numbers (sales × average sale price).

Etan is from quality control and regulatory compliance. Such people are paid to be extremely cautious and risk averse. They are measured on things like negative error rates in production yield and negative complaint rates in usability. As a result, quality and regulatory people like Etan tend to be very controlling, trying to keep the engineers and salespeople from hurting people and creating unnecessary liability.

Lira, from accounting, is highly analytical, of course, and focused on counting the beans. Lira is projecting costs of development and then costs of goods sold, planning budgets, and looking for the return on investment, the sooner the better.

Each human stakeholder tends to zero in on the data that rhymes with their viewpoint.

What can you do?

First, Fine-Tune the Ask

Clearly, there were a lot of wrong turns that the cross-functional team members took each time they met to discuss Res's dream product. But first, before taking any turns at all, they needed to *slow down*. They needed to stop, back up, and get the clarity and details that would help them make an informed decision.

From one perspective, the marching orders from the CEO, the imperative from the regional president, and the pitch from Res might appear straightforward and simple and an obvious progression. Lurking below the surface, however, was the untamed initial ask, which led to a cascade of sloppy asks, yeses, noes, and more asks, all seeking to navigate to a destination that was never made clear in the first place.

Rather than get drawn into Res's ask, which was disguised as a solution to the ask for a blockbuster, the team members should have first tuned in to the *initial* ask from the CEO. They could have learned a lot more from the president and the executive team about appropriate parameters, which would have helped them achieve greater vertical alignment. Within those guardrails, the team really should have considered multiple options and compared them to Res's idea, which would have made it obvious how many details were missing in Res's ask.

Instead, the team members were in a hurry to get rolling, so they skipped over the due diligence up front and then stumbled along trying to fully realize a yes that should have been, at most, a "not yet." As they tried to get from an ill-conceived idea to a decent launch, there was a lot of adjusting along the way and a lot of questioning of the initial decision. Once everything fell apart, nearly every decision looked like an error in retrospect.

But what if the whole thing had gone differently? What if the regional president had stopped up front and tried to fine-tune the CEO's marching order? For example, "Is the ask here really to launch a new blockbuster product this year? Or is the order actually to create steady growth in revenue plus clear progress toward a new blockbuster product soon?"

Or what if the team members had stopped the regional president up front and really tuned in to that ask as stated, "Develop a blockbuster product ready for launch by the end of the year"? They might have said, collectively:

> *"No, that's not possible." Or . . .*

> *"No, that's not allowed." Or . . .*

> *"No, that's not a great idea . . . because it's going to starve resources from very doable things that will be very valuable, such as making a fix to an existing product and other things."*

At the very least, they should have said, "Wait, wait. We need to know a lot more about what we are being asked before we proceed: we need to put some parameters around this ask, some guardrails."

Or what if the team had stopped when Res proposed his idea and really interrogated that ask. Let's remember that Etan (the quality and regulatory guy) and Lira (the accountant) did try to slow down the group to consider some good reasons for a no. Maybe the group would have seriously considered Etan's and Lira's caution if Etan and Lira didn't both have reputations for saying no to every idea.

Instead of listening to Etan and Lira saying no, no, no, the group preferred to go with Res's idea to save the day (but sacrifice the future) with a false set of yes, yes, yes promises. What the group should have done was stop and fine-tune Res's ask:

> *First and foremost:* "What does the market really want? We should be looking at multiple possible products with likely or proven demand."

> *Then:* "What is feasible technically, not just possible? How do we determine, from the outset, that we are designing something for efficient and affordable production and safe use?"

> *Finally:* "Best case, how many do we think we can sell, to whom, over what time frame, and at what cost?"

> "What is the potential for supply chain problems leading to production delays?"

> "What is the potential for production errors leading to service and replacement costs?"

Just imagine if the team members had slowed down up front to get the answers to those questions. They might have decided that they couldn't deliver a blockbuster in one year, but maybe they could deliver a blockbuster in two years; meanwhile, what their customers really wanted was a simple upgrade to one of the company's leading products, which they could deliver in less than a year. Maybe the finance and sales leaders would get together and realize that what they should be doing is looking for another product already in the market and buy it and hire its inventor, as they did with Res two years earlier. That bundle of solutions would have yielded much better outcomes, all in alignment with the CEO's real needs and the regional president's need to fulfill the CEO's needs.

The ask is the time to drill down before you overcommit or, more likely, before you wrongly commit. So much of what we say to each other at work is about asking. Why do we treat our asks—the ones we make and those others make—with so little thought?

A sloppy ask can do a lot of damage. Sometimes the ask is misunderstood: it sounds like more than it is or less than it is, or it sends people off in the wrong direction. Sometimes the ask is not heard at all. It just goes into the ether.

Sometimes people hear the ask and ignore it: "Maybe if I just ignore it, it will go away." I call this "ghosting the ask." This is too common when a person doesn't want to deal with someone else's need or with saying no. The practice is impolite and disrespectful. At the very least, ghosting gives you a reputation for being unresponsive, not a good reputation to have in a high-collaboration environment. Don't be a ghost.

How to Tune In to the Ask

If you want to have more power to make decisions, one of the best things you can do is win a reputation for being highly responsive to people's requests. Tune in to them and engage. That doesn't mean you have to say yes. You can develop a great reputation for being highly responsive by engaging with the ask. Tuning in to the ask is a sign of taking the asker's needs seriously and giving them due consideration.

When somebody is coming to you with a request, think in terms of real influence. Look for opportunities to serve others;

make yourself valuable. Someone is trying to "hire" you to meet their need. Even if you can't do it, tuning in to the ask is step one in building the relationship.

Get in the habit of tuning in to every ask and then whipping it into shape. How do you tame the ask?

- When you are the asker, get really good at clarifying and detailing the ask. Put it all in the form of a simple proposal.

- When you are the person being asked, get really good at helping people fine-tune their asks. Ask questions and take notes—do an intake memo to help them drill down and detail their ask.

Whichever side of the ask you are on, you can turn the ask into a more or less simple proposal. If you think about it, that's what a proposal is—just a very well-formed ask.

The elements of a proposal are:

1. The proposed deliverable

2. The steps along the way

3. The guidelines, parameters, sequence, timing, ownership, and cost of each step

The key is to clarify every aspect accurately and honestly, including the pros and cons; the costs and benefits. Sometimes it's a tiny ask, but you should make sure you know exactly what is needed and what you can provide.

The problem is that most asks don't come in that format.

Not only that, but the nature of some asks and the askers is that if you tell them you want them to put all their micro-requests into the form of a coherent proposal, they'll treat you as if you're crazy and obstructionist, creating a bunch of ridiculous bureaucracy. And they'd have a point.

So, turn every ask into a brief proposal by getting in the habit of doing intake memos. Ask good questions and build a proposal from the inside out. Lawyers do intake memos. So do accountants and doctors. Do you?

The intake memo is a document that professionals create for their own reference to capture and memorialize the particulars of a need a potential client or customer presents to them. Imagine the confidence that askers will gain in your judgment and your promises, your yeses and noes, if you are creating an intake memo, a mutually approved record, for every ask.

All asks great and small deserve an intake memo. Sometimes you'll do it on the back of an envelope or the back of your hand or maybe in a notebook you carry everywhere. Or, maybe you'll start carrying a handheld super-computer on which you can make a note any time anyone makes an ask. Oh. You already do that. Use it.

In an intake memo, you start to gather the information you need as a first step in your due diligence process:

1. What is the date and time, for tracking evolutions in the project?

2. Who is the asker?

3. What is the exact deliverable being requested?

4. What is the delivery date?

5. What are the specifications?

6. What are the resources that will be required?

7. What is the source of authority? Who's asking for it? Who's authorizing it? Has it already been approved? If so, by whom?

8. What are the possible benefits, hidden costs, unsurfaced objections, toes to be stepped on?

The bigger or more complicated the ask, the more information you need to gather. But, often, what seem like small asks end up ballooning into big asks, once you start to delve into the details. That's one of the best reasons to get in the habit of doing an intake memo for every ask, big or small. Finally, share the intake memo with the asker to ensure you're on the same page.

Master the *No*

Lots of people will tell you, "In order to fight overcommitment syndrome, people have to learn how to say no." But the idea that, if somehow you could sugarcoat your no, people would be happier to accept it is just silly. Of course, be polite. But remember this: what will lead to more and more people accepting your no at face value is when you develop a reputation and build a track record for saying no at the right times for the right reasons.

A good no, well decided at the right time, is a huge favor to everybody. It saves everybody a lot of time and trouble down the road, when yes is going to turn out to have been a mistake. People will remember. (See the sidebar "Yes, No, or Not Yet? How to Say It" later in the chapter.)

There's nothing quite like a no executed at the right time. *No*, remember, is all about opportunity cost, freeing up opportunity for good yeses: shutting down or delaying something to make room for something else.

But most people don't know that timing and logic are the keys to delivering a good no. A no can be very sloppy, in very many ways. Just ask the people who relied on Rick, a service technician.

Rick was very much in demand because he could fix anything. Everyone wanted to go to him. But over the years, he'd gotten into a bad habit. He said yes to the things and the people he wanted to, and no to the things he didn't want to do or to people he didn't like. This made Rick feel pretty powerful. But when his boss learned about Rick's selective system, he wasn't happy. The boss implemented a decision-making process, and thereafter, all requests for Rick's help went first through the boss and his process. Meantime, Rick's bad decision making—especially his sloppy noes—lost him a lot of the professional standing and personal power he once had.

Noes end up being sloppy for any number of reasons. The no may come from personal reasons of dislike, as Rick's did, or in dismissal of someone insufficiently important to seek to impress. The no may come because there have been too many yeses and now there is simply no room for a yes.

When people give out sloppy noes, here's what happens: sometimes they get overruled and have to comply anyway, but by now there may be bad feelings. Of course, too many noes are forced upon you by your own overcommitment syndrome, which then causes you to miss out on some great opportunities to add value, develop relationships, and build up real influence.

If the ask was a good idea, but unclear or otherwise not fully developed, then the no might be sloppy because the answer should have been "not yet . . . go back and improve the ask." Even the worst no at least doesn't waste time, energy, and resources spent in the wrong direction. But inaction is a decision nonetheless, depriving you of engagement with the ask and the asker, as well as experience making good decisions.

The very good no is all about timing and the logic of due diligence.

When to Say No

No at work is a way to prevent you and your colleagues from wasting time and attention and, very likely, money and other resources. No is how you protect yourself and others from making bad commitments, dedicating resources trying to do things that *cannot* be done (not possible), are *not allowed* (against the rules), or that on balance, *should not be done* (a bad idea or not the next top priority).

I call these reasons the "no gates," borrowing from the concept of the gate review process, a project management technique dividing projects or initiatives into distinct phases, each of which must be subjected to a review: a "go, no go" decision point, a yes or no. At each gate, certain requirements must be met.

The No Gates

You have to pass the no gates in order to get to yes (giving one or getting one):

1. I simply *cannot* do it. I don't have the skill, knowledge, capacity in time, resources, or energy.

2. I'm *not allowed* to do it. There are procedures, rules, guidelines, or regulations that prohibit it.

3. I *should not* do it. This one is tough because it requires making a real business decision about likelihood of success, potential return on investment, or next top priorities.

The "should not be done" no gate is not always so clear, at least not at first. That's why the answer might be "maybe" or "not yet." In that case, you probably should send the asker back to make a more thorough or more convincing ask or proposal. Maybe you will have some very specific questions that you want the person to answer or objections to address.

If the answer is "not yet," and the asker can't wait—or if it is "no" and they're going to proceed without you—you probably don't want to let this be the end of the relationship. So, what else can you do at this stage?

- If you really think the idea is a bad one, you can try to convince the asker not to do it or to alter their plans. You might be doing them a huge favor. The better your track record of making good judgments, the more you'll be able to have an impact on their plans.

- If you think the idea is fine, but just not for you right now, then maybe you can help them find an alternative go-to person. This could be a chance for you to start creating a backup for yourself and building up another go-to person to extend and strengthen your networks. You will be doing a favor for both parties by putting them together.

- In either case, don't lose the opportunity to make clear all the ways you might add value for each other in the future. Make sure that they understand what you do and that you understand what they do.

Master the *Yes*

Every good no makes room for a better yes.

Yes is positive. Yes signals agreement. Yes is usually good news. Yes should mark the beginning of a collaboration—the next steps in a working relationship. Yes should mean that a well-formed ask was made and carefully considered and that all the no gates have been successfully passed. Yes should mean we are about to embark on a good idea together.

But so often yes is sloppy. It's handled haphazardly or comes in an offhand way—"Yes, of course!"—without a full understanding of what's even been asked. Sometimes, yes is implied through inaction. That happens, in certain situations, when you ignore a request for too long or you fail to shut down a course of action. Yes can be weaponized (as a verb) by those who yes others in order to feign agreement and cut off efforts to convince. When yes is a feigned commitment intended to induce the asker to reasonably rely on the promise, it is actually fraud.

Maybe the ask is not clear and so the yes cannot be clear. Or the yes is made to please in the short term or impress or avoid conflict. Or the yes comes after a series of mediocre or bad noes, so yes just finally seems due in the queue (in other words, for no good reason).

Yes, No, or Not Yet? How to Say It

No at the right time for the right reasons is always a gift, so make it clear: No . . .

. . . I physically cannot do it because I don't have the necessary _____ [experience, skill, knowledge, time, tools, etc.] . . . Allow me to introduce you to another go-to person.

. . . I am not allowed to do it because it is against the _____ [law, rules, procedures, or marching order from my boss] . . . Allow me to recommend a go-to person to learn more about this.

. . . I should not do it, at least right now, because _____ [there are other items higher on my current priority list, *or* I don't think it's a good idea, *or* the ask is still not sufficiently clear] . . . Allow me to introduce you to another go-to person, or perhaps we can return to this discussion at a later date and time.

Remember, you can always say no (or yes, actually) by saying "yes" . . .

The Backlash of the Sloppy Yes

When people make sloppy yeses, they get overcommitted, but this goes way beyond overcommitment syndrome. When you are overcommitted, you miss out on better yeses, so the cost of every sloppy yes multiplies in opportunity cost. Plus, you com-

I can do this in two days . . . or two weeks . . . or two months . . . or two years.

Sometimes the answer is "not yet" . . . and

. . . May I ask you some questions to better understand exactly what you need?

or

. . . Help me understand if I'm the one who can help you meet your needs on time and on spec in this case, or if I need to help you find someone else who can.

Yes, when you say it at the beginning of a collaboration, make it clear: Yes . . .

. . . How can I help you help me help you? What information can I provide about how I do what I do?

or

. . . I'll do *abc* by this date or time, and you do xyz by this date or time; let's talk again for a fifteen-minute check-in at the end of the day Thursday. How does that sound?

mit not just your time but also resources, and often the time of other people (possibly your team, if you are a manager). It's likely to take a while before you realize the yes was not good, and you may well have wasted a bunch of time, energy, and money. And you've likely caused problems that have to be fixed.

The sloppy yes can also leave you susceptible to errors and delays, wasted resources, rework, not to mention project scope creep and role creep. That can happen if the ask was a good idea but unclear and not fully developed. Or if the yes was made with all the available information, but then it was poorly planned. That's like driving in the wrong direction, with a car full of people, wasting all that time, gas, and wear and tear on the vehicle. Sometimes you get a flat tire along the way or get into an accident; then, not only do you have to come all the way back, but you still have to get wherever you should have been going in the first place.

In addition, sloppy yeses are often highly visible, so they are not great for your reputation. You can point fingers and blame others, but that won't be good for your relationships or your reputation. It's certainly no way to build real influence. (See the sidebar "The Yes People.")

Set Up Every Yes for Success

Remember, every good no is there just to set up your great yeses—saying yes to collaboration, saying yes to an opportunity to add value and build a relationship.

Every yes deserves a plan for focused execution. The execution plan is the key to a great yes.

Some yeses are short and sweet, but they still deserve a plan, however short and sweet. Every yes is a commitment, and every commitment deserves to be taken seriously and honored with a good plan and focused execution.

If you have done a really good job tuning in to the ask, doing an intake memo, and framing the ask in terms of the basic elements of a proposal, and seriously considered the no gates, including an ROI analysis, then you should have a pretty good idea of what you are committing to when you say yes. Still, if you are not yet accustomed to working together with the asker—if they are not one of your regular customers—there will be plenty of details to clarify about how you are going to do business together. Don't take the details for granted or you will likely have one small surprise after another.

Yes is the time to really pin down the commitment with a plan of action, especially for a deliverable of any scope. How do you move the conversation from yes to a plan? By asking the platinum question: *"How can I help you help me help you?"* In other words, what ground rules might you need to establish for working together? What will be your cadence of communication, where, when, and how? In terms of the work: Who is going to do what, where, why, when, and how? You need to agree on the sequence, timing, and ownership of all the steps. End every conversation by clarifying who owns which next steps and scheduling your next follow-up conversation. The punch line is always the next steps. Planning is the key to successful execution. Plan the work so you can work your plan.

Make Better Choices, Early and Often

Imagine if you and all your collaboration partners could start making better, more intentional decisions about how you all allocate your time and energy. Every single yes means there's more work to be done. The chapters that come next—"Work Smart," and "Finish What You Start" are all about execution.

The Yes People

Watch out for the classic types who are very uncareful in how they say yes. And don't be one yourself.

The Entangler

The entangler seen in chapter 2's bad attitudes is often well meaning, but gets too involved in your details and tries to involve you in too many of theirs. It's as if they are lonely and want you to keep them company. They often present themselves as an ever-ready helper—a sidekick or someone looking for a sidekick. The entangler wants two people doing the job of one person—two hands, one hammer. They can consume a lot of your time and be hard to untangle from.

The Generous Fool

The generous fool is the person, always well meaning, who wants desperately to be of service, but is not very good at it. They promise to do things for you that they are simply unable to do or that they are not allowed to do. So they'll likely take up too much of your time, give you the impression that your needs are being taken care of, but ultimately disappoint you. Generous fools might think they are meeting your needs, until the very end when they deliver and you discover that they didn't meet your needs at all. All the while, you have missed the opportunity to engage with someone who could help you. So, be nice to the generous fools, but don't work with them. Be generous, but don't be a fool.

The Overpromiser

Overpromisers sometimes look like the generous fool, because they often come from a good place as they aim to please. They love the feeling at the moment of the promise, like giving a kid cotton candy for dinner. Overpromisers think they are taking the easy way out on the front end by not doing the due diligence. But before long, they pay a big price, and so will the people around them. Sometimes overpromisers are big talkers. They love to impress in a meeting or when they are talking to the boss, a customer, or another big shot. Sometimes, overpromisers go rogue. They want to be helpers or heroes or have a fun adventure. Of course, rogues may also tend to ditch their rogue commitments at the last minute.

If you have a tendency to overpromise, remember that the short-term gratification for you and the person you make a promise to will soon be far overshadowed by the negative impact of overpromising: failure to deliver, delays, mistakes, and relationship damage.

CHAPTER SUMMARY

- Take other people's needs seriously by giving every ask its due diligence.

- Make better choices sooner.
  - Every good choice now will save everybody so much time and trouble later and will make others more confident in your choices in the future.

- Tune in to every ask with an intake memo.
  - Ask good questions and build a proposal from the inside out. Use this approach to guide your own asking, too.

- Learn when to say no (or not yet).
  - Here are the "no gates":

    I simply cannot do it. I don't have the skill, knowledge, capacity in time, resources, or energy.

    I'm not allowed to do it. There are procedures and rules that prohibit it.

    I should not do it. It's just, on balance, not a good idea or my next priority. The answer might be "not yet."

- Learn how to say yes.
  - Every yes deserves a focused execution plan.
  - Establish ground rules for working together, a cadence of communication, and a clear sequence, timing, and ownership of all the steps.

5

Work Smart

Petra and Michelle are colleagues in supply chain management at an aerospace company. Petra had just returned from lunch when she overheard Michelle on the phone. "Yes, OK. I'll take care of it," Michelle said before hanging up. Then she murmured aloud, *"That's not my job!"*

With an imploring look, she glanced over at Petra and said, "I'm already overloaded with my own work. I don't have time to help them do their job too! Petra, I don't know how you do it."

Petra is a total go-to person. She gets more work done, better and faster, than anybody else in their purchasing group. In addition, she somehow finds time to train and mentor less experienced colleagues.

Petra responded with a little smile, "Well, maybe that *could* be part of your job."

Said Michelle, "What?! I don't think I can work any harder than I am already."

Petra looked at her colleague thoughtfully. "That's just it, Michelle," she said. "It's not just about working hard. You have to *work smart*."

It's All about Changing Your Mindset

No matter how good you get at setting up your yeses for success, still, with every yes, your work pile grows.

If, like Michelle, you only work hard, you'll only get over-committed, resentful, tired, and under siege. That's no way to be a go-to person. So, you'd better work smart:

- *First, professionalize everything you do.* Whatever your job is, make sure you do it really, really well. Some organizations have effective, timely training to prepare you—and good systems and tools to support you—for every task, responsibility, and project you might undertake as part of your job. If your employer does not, then you'd better create your own.

- *Second, specialize in whatever you do best.* That means focusing as much of your work time as possible doing the things you already do really well. That's why, ironically, there is actually a lot of wisdom hidden in "that's not my job"—despite the phrase's bad reputation. Know what specialties you want to be known for. The more work you do in your specialties, the better your outcomes. Every minute you spend on the things you do very well adds more value than a minute spent on something that is *not* your specialty.

- *Third, keep expanding your repertoire.* Sometimes, as Petra advised Michelle, it's wise to consider doing the thing that's "not my job." After all, you don't want to specialize so much that you get stuck in a pigeonhole. So be on the lookout for opportunities to add a *new* specialty.

Let's take these one at a time.

Professionalize Everything You Already Do

Some organizations are great when it comes to providing effective, timely training in best practices, as well as good systems and tools for every task, responsibility, and project. Anytime there is a gap in those kinds of resources related to any of your work, do not just assume you'll figure it out along the way. Instead, you need to be very purposeful about creating your own.

When Michelle first started her job in the purchasing group, she had to jump right in. There was a backlog of work throughout the supply chain—from vendors all the way to the end users in research, engineering, and production—and there were new buying requests coming in every day. Other than a basic orientation, there was no formal training. There were no work instructions, templates, or checklists. The person she had replaced had his own system, but that wasn't much of a system. At first, she started looking through his old emails and work product to try to build a system. But there wasn't much she could use. After all, that's why she'd been hired to replace him.

Like everyone else in her group, she was told to shadow someone more experienced. So, Michelle pulled up a chair and sat with Roberto for a week or so, watching him use the two basic computer systems. The first was for managing incoming requisitions to purchase things like parts, supplies, tools, and services. The second was a vendor management system for choosing the appropriate vendor and submitting the purchase order. Michelle picked up the basics of working the two computer systems. But she noticed that, from one transaction to the next, very little happened in the same way. Some required less information, some required more; some orders were simple, whereas some had additional steps—approvals or competitive bids, incoming quality inspection, special shipping, and so on.

Whenever Michelle asked Roberto, "Why?" he said, "Well, that's how you have to do it for this person." Finally, Roberto said, "Every vendor and every customer is a special case. That's why it's not as easy a job as it looks. You'll get used to it."

Michelle struggled to get used to it and to keep up. Then Petra joined the purchasing group. What a gift! In Petra's previous job in supply chain management at a larger aerospace company, she'd enjoyed a really good training program, systems, and tools. She'd acquired all kinds of best practices for learning and documenting the varying requirements and idiosyncrasies of her internal customers as well as her vendors. Indeed, it turned out that many of the vendors in her new company were the same as those she'd dealt with in her last job.

One of her best practices was to interview (by phone and written questionnaire) each new customer and vendor, and to create a process flowchart, work instructions, and ordering templates for each person. She taught her customers (and vendors) to use their template whenever working with her, which they learned to love because it made transactions go faster and better. Then, if Petra needed to communicate with another vendor to get a competing bid, for example, or with someone in shipping and receiving, she had these tools at her disposal to help her create clarity in every aspect of the transaction, even if it was above and beyond the job of just processing requisitions and placing orders.

Petra took Michelle under her wing and shared her best practices, copies of her flowcharts, work instructions, and ordering templates. Soon, others noticed and started using Petra's approach and tools as well. When Roberto, whom Michelle had been shadowing, started using Petra's best practices and job aids, he remarked how helpful they would have been when he was learning the job himself.

That's the power of professionalization.

Three Keys to Professionalization

To professionalize any task, responsibility, or project, do these three things:

1. Identify, study, and follow the proven *best practices* in your field and in your organization. Turn them into standard operating procedures.

2. Bank and reuse *repeatable solutions*, rather than reinventing the wheel every time. These are the solutions to recurring problems that naturally emerge when you regularly use your standard operating procedures.

3. Use whatever *job aids* you can find—such as work instructions, checklists, templates, and prior work products.
   These are the things that will help you systematically follow those best practices and use those repeatable solutions.
   Once you get comfortable with the basics, build some job
   aids of your own.

Best practices. Any task, responsibility, or project can usually
be done in a number of different ways. What is the best way? Best
for speed? Best for quality? Best for cost? Best for beauty? Best for
what?

Think of anything you are really good at. Playing baseball?
House painting? Accounting? Moving boxes? There may be
many different ways to field a ground ball, but the best practice is
surely to bend your knees, put your glove to the ground in line
with the trajectory of the ball, and have your other hand just
behind the glove to back it up. The same goes for painting a
house. Best practice is to first scrape, then caulk, then prime,
and then paint—one or two coats—using rollers up and down and
brushes for "cutting in." The same with keeping accounts and
with moving boxes. There are lots of ways to do things, but it's
good to know the best practice.

Best practices are methods that are currently the most effective and efficient techniques for accomplishing an outcome.
Sometimes best practices are obvious. Too often they hide below
the radar. Somebody has mastered a best practice and nobody
else knows about it. Or not enough people know about it. Too
often people figure things out on their own instead of looking
around for people who have already mastered the best practices and are documenting them—turning them into standard

operating procedures and making job aids like checklists or work instructions.

Repeatable solutions. Once Michelle started using Petra's templates, she sometimes found herself bumping up against the same few problems again and again. So, she began having conversations with her colleagues about their experiences. These were punctuated with a lot of "That's how you do it?" and "Here's how I do it" and "Your way is better" and "That didn't work when I tried it." Michelle was amazed at how many solutions and opportunities to improve systems were hiding just below the surface.

For example, there were many instances of people asking each other the same questions and different people having different dimensions of the answers. So, Michelle and Petra started keeping a running list of "Answers to Frequently Asked Questions." That document was filled with repeatable solutions and served as a fine job aid for just about everybody in the purchasing group. One of the most common failures with one vendor was successful shipping, so Michelle borrowed Petra's solution of using a credit card to pay FedEx or UPS to ship from that particular vendor. Of course, she had to use that solution selectively, but Michelle was glad to have it up her sleeve when it came to sticky delivery situations.

Job aids. Finally, when it comes to professionalizing everything you do, job aids may be the hardest working piece in the puzzle. All of your checklists, work instructions, and templates are what allow you to systematically follow the best practices and use the repeatable solutions.

Besides helping you get your work done quickly and accurately, job aids also ensure you stay aligned with your boss in how you do your work. And as Petra found with her ordering templates, which she individualized for each client, they help you educate your customers and manage their expectations by making your processes clear and transparent. Perhaps best of all, your job aids will help you train new go-to people to support you and/or back up your role. That way, they, too, can become professionalized specialists, contributing to a virtuous cycle.

How do you build job aids? Every time you fine-tune a task or responsibility, you capture in writing your new and improved best practices. And you maintain updated standard operating procedures and turn them into checklists (step-by-step instructions), or another sort of job aid that can be easily understood and used—not just for your use—by others, too. (See the sidebar "Turn Your Best Practices into a Shareable Job Aid.")

I'm amazed at how often high performers make their own job aids, but never share them with others. Whenever I find one of those people, I tell them, "Share it!" Being the best source of information on any important task or responsibility is a great way to become the epitome of a go-to person.

Of course, well-developed organizations have always used standard operating procedures based on current best practices for as many tasks, responsibilities, and projects as they can. That's the key to scalability. Just imagine running, say, a chain of restaurants without having the same basic layout, menus, staffing, marketing, and so on. If the chain's leaders are smart, these procedures live in the form of job aids like work instructions, checklists, templates, and scripts.

If your organization has good standard operating procedures and corresponding job aids, master them. But also pay attention to all the things you do for which there are currently no identified best practices turned into standard operating procedures; and therefore no readily available work instructions, templates, or examples of prior work products.

I've seen waiters create scripts for themselves to improve their engagement and service to dining customers, and to increase their sales of the day's specials, the high-priced wines, and desserts. I've seen building inspectors use the same checklist of every possible thing that might go wrong to inspect buildings of all shapes and sizes. I've seen software engineers build one new package on top of another, overwriting code from a previous program to create a new one. I've seen regulatory affairs managers start a new compliance submission, not from scratch, but by overwriting a document containing a previous submission. I've seen marketing professionals start with the layout of one ad to inspire the next.

Job aids are truly the gift that keeps on giving—to you and your colleagues and clients:

- *Job aids keep you from getting rusty.* Job aids can help you get up to speed more quickly with tasks you don't do often or haven't done in a while. If this is a task, responsibility, or project that you do only periodically, then it's doubly important to capture all of the lessons you learn when you are deep in it. You don't want to have to dust off your memory the next time. You don't want to relearn the same things you already learned in the last go-around. Job aids such as work instructions, checklists, and comparable work products will

Turn Your Best Practices into a Shareable Job Aid

Here's how to create a shareable job aid:

1. Write out step-by-step instructions for the task, from memory or whatever else is your current best source. Break each task into its component steps and break each step into a series of concrete actions.

2. Perform the task, very slowly, keeping one eye on the instructions you prepared. As you perform the task, make corrections and additions to your step-by-step instructions.

3. Perform the task again, very slowly, and make further corrections and additions. Include as many details on each step—and in between each step—as you can think of.

4. Write a new draft of the step-by-step instructions in the form of a checklist.

jump-start your performance the next time you tackle the same responsibility or a comparable project. So find, create, and use your job aids. Don't let yourself get rusty.

- *Job aids keep you from going on autopilot.* At the other end of the spectrum are those tasks that you do over and over again, sometimes daily and even multiple times a day. Job aids such as step-by-step checklists will keep you from

5. Ask someone else to try using your checklist to guide them and see if it works for them. Get their suggestions for further corrections and additions.

6. Going forward, use this checklist to guide you in completing your task and also for making notes along the way. Remember, the key is actually *using* the checklists. You have to say "check" or actually check off each item on the checklist as you go along. Make clarifying notes in the margins of the checklists as you use them.

The same goes for work products: every time you complete a tangible result, capture that work product and keep it in a *library of work products* that can later be repurposed—not just by you—but also by others.

If others can understand and use your job aids and work products, then you will have an easier time understanding and using them later, too, when they are less fresh in your experience. Capturing your work isn't about just thinking ahead to your own utility and convenience. It's also about helping people help you help them—making it easier for people to understand what you do and how you can do it for them.

just doing those things mindlessly, by rote, or going on autopilot.

When you do anything mindlessly, that's when mistakes happen, quality suffers, or opportunities are overlooked. You might start to think you can multitask with another task or responsibility. Pretty soon, your error rate goes up. When that happens, it's time to slow down, take out your instructions and checklists, follow them step by step, and check them off one by one. That's how your job aids can keep you focused and serve as quality control. They are tools of mindfulness to get you back to dotting your i's and crossing your t's as effectively as possible. Don't let yourself go on autopilot.

But, sometimes, rather than preventing autopilot from kicking in, all those checklists and other job aids can actually trigger autopilot, especially when you use the same tools repeatedly. After a while, they start to turn into wallpaper. Rather than using them as tools for mindfulness, you start to tune them out and ignore them.

If that happens, it's time to change things up. A simple example is to take your checklist and rearrange it. Do things in a different order. Or make a set of micro-steps within each item on the checklist (a set of checklists within the checklist). The idea is to make yourself (and others) stop and think; if the checklist is not making you stop and think, then you need to rearrange it.

- *Job aids help you build up other go-to people.* Sharing your job aids (detailing best practices and repeatable solutions) will help you increase the productive capacity of others and improve their ability to rely on you with greater confidence and work with you more effectively.

  That's how you build up other go-to people. When you're overcommitted and must say no to a customer yourself, ask some of your go-to people to fill in for you. You know they'll do a good job because they already have all your job aids and work product samples. These will help get them on board, up to speed, and backing you up faster. That's a positive you can deliver for your internal customers, even if you are overcommitted and unavailable. And it's a positive you can deliver for backup go-to people because you are building them up and giving them an opportunity to add value and become more and more of a go-to person themselves.

- *Job aids help you educate your cross-functional collaborators.* Your instruction sheets and checklists show your collaborators how you do business, while at the same time teaching them how to do business with you.

  When you are working with your internal customers in other teams, functions, or departments, they often have lots of blind spots about what you do, how you do it, and how best to work effectively with you. Sometimes they might wonder, "Why are you asking me all these questions?" And "What's taking so long?" If they don't fully understand what it takes for you (and your team) to complete a task, responsibility, or project on your end, that might breed frustration and bad feelings.

  So, use your job aids to create greater alignment with your cross-functional partners. Help them understand exactly what steps are required for you to meet their needs. The better they understand your job as it relates to them, the more likely they will see opportunities to help you help them—and the better you can work together to fine-tune your systems for the best outcome, faster, all while improving the process of working together.

Specialize in Whatever You Do *Best*

Put a laser focus on what you do best. Once you've mastered professionalizing your job, make sure you develop and fine-tune your specialty, which means that sometimes saying "that's really not my specialty" is a pretty good reason to say no. And it sounds a lot better than "that's not my job." It's all part of working smart.

Let's return to Michelle. Once she began working with Petra to professionalize her job—streamlining best practices, documenting repeatable solutions, and creating and using all kinds of job aids—Michelle zeroed in on what she was good at doing and then what she was *best* at doing.

She began by specializing, first, in dealing with certain vendors who had particularly complex ordering-documentation processes because of the very technical nature of the parts they supplied. Dealing with those complex transactions led her to specialize, next, in serving the research scientists who were at the very edge of innovation.

Those two things were a good mix of expertise for Michelle to develop, because they reflected two long-standing abilities Michelle had fine-tuned over many years and in a number of jobs: complex technical documentation (she'd been educated as an electrical engineer) and communicating effectively with very technically sophisticated, mad-scientist types. Honing her specialty—serving those research scientists by being great at understanding and then placing those highly technical orders—gave new meaning to Michelle's work, helping her stay focused and set priorities. And it illuminated her value to her purchasing group.

Do you have a specialty? What do you do best? What are those tasks, responsibilities, or projects that are really in your wheelhouse? This is the work where you know just what to do and just how to do it, and what might go wrong and how, usually, to avoid it. You also know on a deep level what it takes, in the microcosm of your specialty, to ask others to "help me help you help me." You know how to optimize your productive capacity, maximize your impact, and dramatically increase the ROI on your work.

What's more, you are pretty certain that every minute you spend on one of your specialties, you will add more value, better and faster, than someone who doesn't have your specialty—or than you would by spending any particular minute doing something that is *not* one of your specialties. That's true, whether you are digging ditches or practicing surgery.

"I do these highly specialized procedures, correcting birth defects in newborns—chest, abdominal, urological," says Naomi, a neonatal surgeon. "I've done thousands of these procedures. Every one of them is unique, but every one of them is also the same." Who would you want to operate on your baby who has a birth defect? Not the surgeon who hasn't done these procedures over and over again. That's for sure.

Or what if you need to dig a ditch? "I've been digging ditches for a long time," says George, a longtime program manager for a mining company. "I started just running a jackhammer on a crew. I graduated to running larger machinery. I've broken ground on hundreds of digs. At one time or another, I've done every stage of just about every kind of dig."

When you need to dig a ditch, who are you going to call? Certainly not the person who hasn't done every stage of just about every kind of dig. Or the person who knows only how to run the jackhammer for a basic job.

True specialists not only professionalize everything they do, but also have so much experience that they've collected memories and examples of successful outcomes, successful procedures, successful work products along the way for every recurring responsibility or project, so that they always have something to work from or from which to imitate or at least extrapolate.

If you are a specialist, you also know how to use your standard operating procedures, repeatable solutions, job aids, and prior successful outcomes in order to teach the colleagues with whom you collaborate enough about what you do to help them help you help them. Meanwhile, do not fall into the trap of being great at just the aspects of the job you like and slacking on the aspects you don't like or consider ancillary. This is a very common mistake, and there are infinite examples, often to do with paperwork. George from the mining company says, "Some of the guys are great at running large machinery, but they slack on doing the safety checks, or the shift handoff checklist. I tell them, sorry guys, that's part of your job too. If you don't do that stuff, you are letting people down."

Another classic example is the salesperson who loves to sell but fails to dot the i's and cross the t's when it comes to sales activity reports, lead tracking, and even correct preparation of sales orders. Or the research scientist or development engineer who loves technology but hates all the documentation necessary for quality control, regulatory, transfer to production, and so on.

Keep Expanding Your Repertoire

Working smart means going beyond professionalizing your job and beyond being a specialist in your job. You also need to grow, change, and expand to make yourself even more indispensable. How? By steadily increasing, expanding, and professionalizing your repertoire of specialties into areas *beyond* your job. The more specialties you have, the more of your time you'll be able to devote to high-impact value adding—working in your wheelhouse—and the less time you will spend doing things that are not your job (because you've made those things a specialty). Remember, work that is not your job is where most of the new opportunities for expanding your expertise are hiding.

Whenever I hear somebody say (or suspect they might be thinking), "That's not my job," I know it might be bad news or good news, because:

- If this is not a go-to person, then they probably mean, "I don't want to do this" or "I shouldn't have to do this" or "You can't make me." In short, they are resisting the extra work. That's bad news.

- On the other hand, if this is a go-to person, they may well mean simply, "That's not something that I can already do very well, very fast, with confidence that I am using established best practices and the experience to avoid unnecessary errors and delays."

   That's good news. Because what they are really saying is "I have my specialties, and this is not one of them." It sounds as if, when it comes to their specialties, they do great work and are probably great to work with. If somehow you get them to say yes anyway, even though it's not one of their specialties, you are on notice: it's going to take them some time to climb that learning curve to meet this need for you.

When you find yourself thinking, "That's not my job" (don't say it!), stop and be honest with yourself: Are you just resisting work? If that's you, knock it off. Or are you only trying to work smart? When is the right time to say, "I'm so sorry, but that's really not one of my specialties"? And when do you say, instead, "That's not one of my specialties . . . yet. But I'd love the chance to add this to my repertoire. Be warned, I'm new to this."

Again, it is precisely among all those things that are as yet not your job where all the new opportunities are hiding.

Recall how Petra encouraged Michelle to consider what wasn't "her job" *as something that could be part of her job.* When Michelle stopped to think about it, she saw Petra's point. By professionalizing her work—documenting and resourcing her process maps, work instructions, and templates for each customer and vendor—she was able to really figure out what she was best at: processing those complex high-tech orders for the most sophisticated research scientists. Because those orders often required special packing and shipping arrangements as well, Michelle developed a whole set of contacts, tools, and techniques for shipping delicate machinery as well as dangerous materials.

By doing what wasn't her job (helping the research scientists prepare complex requisitions and assisting the logistics, shipping, and receiving team to arrange for special packaging and transportation of the machinery and materials), Michelle had seriously expanded her repertoire of specialties. Michelle says, "Once I realized, working with Petra, how much better and faster I could do the job, and really master working with different vendors and different customers, the work became much more manageable. And that allowed me to expand and get really good at something else. I've been adding one new responsibility after another by professionalizing every aspect of my work."

When "That" Is Not Your Job

Despite all the advantages of adding to your repertoire, you still need to choose very carefully before saying yes or no to a new task, responsibility, or project.

Sometimes it really shouldn't be your job. Not all opportunities are equally promising. The least promising fall into two main categories:

- *The wild-goose chase.* These are fruitless tasks that are often time consuming and sometimes difficult time wasters that are usually not even much fun. Keep your eyes peeled for the wild-goose chase and do whatever you can to avoid it.

  How do you know a wild-goose chase when you see one? Sometimes it seems obvious, as when somebody asks you to do something that seems nearly impossible. But don't mistake something difficult and ambitious—say, sending a rocket to the moon—with something that's not possible. Something difficult and ambitious might prove to be a game-changing opportunity for you.

One shortcut might be the reputation of the asker. Has this person wasted your time before? Or that of others? Still, prejudging a colleague's requests based on reputation or even your own experience with them might get *you* a reputation for being uncooperative or cliquish (as in, "I won't work with certain people"). And you might miss out on a great opportunity.

The number-one common denominator of the wild-goose chase in the real world is the half-baked ask: if the ask comes in early and then gets revised iteratively, then you are likely to go off in one direction, then another, and then another, without accomplishing much. Sometimes those projects just go away altogether; it becomes clear they shouldn't be undertaken at all. Other times, they are revised and mature into good projects. Either way, the early-stage work proves a fruitless waste of time.

- *You are really the wrong person for this task.* There is a will to prepare, and you are not a lawyer, but a dentist. Or there are braces to install, and you are a lawyer, not an orthodontist. Or there are a hundred heavy boxes to move from one side of the warehouse to the other, but you are a file clerk and don't even know how to drive a forklift.

  In some cases, it would be ridiculous for you to try to do the task yourself. But the great thing about go-to-ism is that, increasingly, if you are a go-to person with real influence, then you have a lot of good customers, and you know where to find go-to people or potential people you can nurture. You know who's who and where to find them, so you can make the introduction and be the connector, which by itself is a service. If you are a go-to person, then your introductions will carry more weight (see more about finding and building go-to people in chapter 8). That ties back—once again—to the importance of building your network and making yourself indispensable by being known as someone who connects talented go-to people to each other.

Sometimes maybe it should be your job. What about times when, yes, you'd probably do well to decide that something seemingly outside your job actually should be part of your job? There are three primary instances:

1. *Somebody's got to do it—and it might as well be you (at least sometimes).* I'm not talking here about tasks ancillary to your primary responsibility but still part of your job, like the heavy machine operators' safety checks and shift handoff checklists, or the neonatal surgeon who washes her own hands.

   I'm talking about the tasks that come up regularly or every so often and belong to no one, but somebody's got to do them—one-off errands. The reasons to sometimes do the occasional one-off errands: good workplace citizenship, teamwork, humility, and sacrifice. And don't forget relationship ROI. People notice, and they appreciate and remember it. For example:

   - Not being the office cleaning service, but perhaps emptying the garbage midweek when it overflows

   - Not repairing office equipment, but knowing how to troubleshoot a paper jam

- Not being the office caterer, but perhaps making the coffee when you come in first

- Not being the office manager, but bringing in the mail or opening a box of supplies when you see them

- Not being a trainer, but taking the time to teach a colleague how to do something new on the computer

Do be careful: you do not want to become that would-be go-to person who jumps at every chance. You won't become a go-to person but, rather, the office gofer.

2. *The job is a close cousin to your specialty.* These are often the most natural and easy opportunities to add to your repertoire. This is the neonatal surgeon specializing in chest, abdominal, and urological procedures who learns a new way to do a procedure using new technology or adds an ENT (ear, nose, and throat) procedure to her bag of tricks. This is the ditchdigger who learns to drive a newer and bigger piece of heavy equipment or dig a new and different kind of ditch. This is the waiter who learns to fill in for the hostess and greet customers in the front of the restaurant. These are the jobs that are usually a good fit with your other responsibilities and relatively easy to add to your repertoire of specialties. It makes sense to do them.

3. *The job presents a brand-new opportunity to truly expand your repertoire—or even take on an additional career or change careers.* It's always a good idea to branch out and build new knowledge, skills, wisdom, relationships, experiences, best practices, tools, work products, and repeatable solutions.

Mastering brand-new specialties is how you truly diversify your opportunities to add value. Some new specialties are easier to add than others. Most require some amount of up-to-speed training. Some require going back to school. This is the restaurant waiter who decides to move from the front of the house to the back, the kitchen. He needs to learn how to cook first. This is the ditchdigger who decides to go into heavy machinery maintenance. He needs to learn how to be a mechanic. This is the neonatal surgeon who decides she's going to start operating on adults.

Or, suppose you are a lawyer and decide you want to be a dentist. Or you are a dentist and decide you want to become a lawyer. Or, perhaps, you decide you will use your training as a dentist in your newly acquired legal profession—say, by focusing on dental malpractice cases, representing dentists, or even suing dentists. My favorite example is Dr. Eric Ploumis, DDS, Esq., in Brooklyn, New York: he is a dentist who decided to study law. That in itself is not the most unusual thing. But Ploumis neither sues nor defends dentists. Rather, he continues to practice dentistry in one office and law in the other. Patients or clients proceed through one door to the law office where they may discuss contracts or instead go to his dental office to have their teeth treated.

How to Expand Your Repertoire

When it comes to expanding your repertoire of specialties, be systematic.

Don't be daunted, but don't be totally undaunted either. Let's say you just got what appears to be a pretty great new assignment with a promising new internal customer. What if you've never done anything quite like this before? What if the thought of it brings out all of your worst fears about your abilities? Don't be intimidated. This is a chance to learn and grow.

But you also don't want to be naïve or arrogant about your abilities. You'd be surprised how often some people, when taking on a new task or assignment, make the mistake of thinking, "How much could there be to this anyway?" Usually, the answer is, "Much more than you might think." So, don't underestimate what you're being asked to do.

Do not try to figure out the new job all on your own. You don't have to wing it alone and try to pull off this new thing without anybody being any the wiser. That approach is for rookies.

No matter what you do, make it knowledge work. Some experts will tell you that knowledge work is about *what* you do. If your tasks, responsibilities, and projects require an especially high level of training, education, and certification (like a doctor, an engineer, or a teacher), then it is knowledge work. Whereas if your job does not require that kind of learning (like digging a ditch, for example), then it is *not* knowledge work.

I disagree.

In our research, we see people every day doing work that doesn't seem to require particularly esoteric knowledge, but nonetheless they are highly intentional about leveraging information, technique, and perspective in everything they do. (I've also seen plenty of people performing classic knowledge work jobs who are notably not thoughtful in their day-to-day performance.)

By our definition, knowledge work isn't only about what you do, but is very much about *how* you do what you do. That's where learning in plain sight comes into play. If you are highly intentional about asking for help and then leveraging that information, technique, and perspective in everything you do, then you are doing knowledge work, even if you're digging a ditch.

What does that really mean? It means, in everything you do, keep an open mind, suspend judgment, question your assumptions, and seek out the information you need. Then study, practice, and contemplate in order to build your stored knowledge base and skill set. Think of the smartest person you know. That person is almost certainly also one of the most voracious learners you know. The biggest mistake that keeps people from getting smarter is thinking that being smart is a fixed status, rather than a dynamic process.

The best thing you can do when acquiring any new knowledge or skill is to start by pretending you don't know anything about it (or at least take note that you don't know everything about it). Then ask yourself: What knowledge, skill, and wisdom would really help me with this new task or responsibility? What information do I need to study? What do I need to memorize or practice again and again? Repetition is often the key to success.

So, be a knowledge worker. Go out of your way to learn, learn, learn at every step, and leverage what you are learning in everything you do.

Learn in plain sight. When you take on something new, don't set yourself up for failure by thinking, "I don't want to be caught learning in plain sight on this because that might diminish people's confidence in me and my work." There is no need to be a surreptitious learner.

Anybody with any experience learning things knows that active learners tend to be the ones who know the most. When you learn in plain sight, smart colleagues will have more confidence in you, not less. Be 1,000 percent transparent to accelerate your learning curve. Ask around and get someone to mentor you in the skill you want to acquire. Ask a lot of really good questions. Inquire about current best practices so you can find them, learn them, build standard operating procedures, and adopt them. Find out about recurring problems and repeatable solutions so you can have them at the ready. Ask about existing job aids like work instructions, checklists, and best of all, examples of similar or related prior work product from which you can learn, imitate, and extrapolate.

Then make it clear at every step that you are actively learning and practicing this new task, responsibility, or project—this new knowledge, skill, and wisdom—in parallel with the work you already do in your current job. Keep asking good questions of good people along the way as you build up best practices, repeatable solutions, and job aids.

Don't reinvent the wheel. Lots of people end up reinventing the wheel when learning something new simply because they didn't realize the wheel had already been invented.

Maybe you've had this experience yourself. You get halfway through a task, responsibility, or project—or all the way through it—and then you realize, "This has already been done before! Why didn't somebody tell me?" The question you should be asking yourself is, "Why didn't *you* investigate the matter before plunging in?"

Remember where we started: professionalize everything you do. That's also how you plunge into something new: look for established best practices, repeatable solutions, and job aids (especially prior successful work products). Most of the new tasks, responsibilities, projects, and problems you encounter at work, though new to you, will probably not be matters of first impression. Almost always, you can assume, this has been done before. Some people have done it better than others. Some have done it best. That's why it's a best practice. Too often, best practices hide below the radar in organizations.

Smart organizations are always looking below the radar to find those best practices and make them available to everybody. Whenever best practices are identified, they should be turned into standard operating procedures, and they should be required learning for people in the organization and supported systematically with high-quality training and job aids.

Working Smart—and Even Smarter

As you build each set of best practices, repeatable solutions, and job aids, you are building your repertoire of services and products—your specialties.

The services and products that you have the most experience with are those you are likely to do the fastest and best. These are the services and products you've had a chance to road test. These are your specialties, the ones you want to be known for as you build your brand as a go-to person.

You want more and more people coming to you for these services and products, those you are already best prepared to deliver, those for which you have developed strong tools and procedures. When your repeatable solutions become the established solutions, and you are clearly happy to see them proliferate, you will find yourself becoming a de facto leader of an organic team forming around you and your repertoire. That's a good thing for your superiors to notice: it's often the path to a swifter promotion and more official authority.

Keep building your repertoire, but remember that the busier you are and the heavier your workload, the more you need to focus on systematic execution. Don't try to be a juggler. You are not really working smart unless you finish what you start.

CHAPTER SUMMARY

- "That's not my job" sometimes really means . . .
  - "That's not something that I can already do very well, very fast, with confidence that I am using established best practices and the experience to avoid unnecessary errors and delays."
- Professionalize everything you do:
  1. Identify, study, and follow best practices, as opposed to "I figured it out along the way" and "This is how I do it."
  2. Bank and reuse repeatable solutions, rather than reinventing the wheel.
  3. Build and use job aids.

- Specialize in whatever you do best.

  - Know what specialties you want to be known for. Every minute you spend adds more value than a minute spent on something that is not your specialty.

- Keep expanding your repertoire.

  - Look for opportunities to add a new specialty. Learn in plain sight and accelerate your learning curve. Professionalize every new specialty: best practices, repeatable solutions, and job aids.

6

Finish What You Start

I once was asked to evaluate and coach a mid-level insurance company executive I'll call "Juggler." Juggler was so busy with so many responsibilities and projects, she was becoming a bottleneck—always working on things, but not finishing them. Her boss and colleagues were starting to complain.

When I appeared at Juggler's door for our scheduled meeting, she was staring intently at her computer. She hadn't yet noticed me, but her phone rang. Without looking away from the screen, Juggler answered the call on speaker: "I'm trying to finish up a calculation and I've got a meeting in a few minutes. What's up?"

I heard the caller say, "Sorry. I thought we had a call scheduled for right now." Juggler responded, "Shoot. You're right. I'm double-booked." By now, Juggler had noticed me and gestured for me to come in and take a seat in her office.

The caller laughed, "Aren't you always double-booked? We can reschedule."

Juggler said, "Thanks. Send me an email. Sorry. Talk to you soon." She disconnected the call and looked up at me.

I said, "Do you need a few minutes?"

Juggler said, "Don't worry. Things are always like this. I've got so much going on. I'm always juggling."

Once we got the interview going, she was eager to tell me all about that impressive workload. There was a whiteboard on Juggler's office wall, with a long list of projects and responsibilities. I was thinking, "Ah, those are all the projects on which you are holding up your colleagues."

"Tell me more about your role on project Q," I inquired. "Tell me more about project J." And so on. Juggler had a lot to say about each project, but I still couldn't tell what she was actually doing.

Finally, I said, "OK. You arrive at work. You have a cup of coffee. Then what do you do—first, second, third?"

Juggler turned the computer screen toward me and showed me a double- and triple-booked schedule, with meetings and conference calls, plus a task manager with overflowing to-do items clearly rolling over from day to day.

I said, "But, which of those to-do items have you actually gotten done today?"

Juggler was at a loss. "I've been so busy all day, but I don't even know what I've gotten done. Did you ever have one of those days?" I suspected that was how a lot of her days turned out.

Just then her mobile phone started buzzing, the computer was pinging, and the desk phone was ringing. Juggler said, "Give me just a minute, please, will you?"

One minute turned into another and another. There was something relatively urgent that Juggler needed to deal with, so we wrapped up our meeting and agreed to schedule a follow-up.

It's not hard to see that Juggler is very busy. But she lacks the focus that would allow her to finish what she starts. Like so many people, Juggler spends way too much time at work awash in a tidal wave of emails; fielding interruptions of low importance; fielding interruptions of high importance (firefighting); attending too many mediocre meetings; and in the midst of all that, trying to squeeze in time to somehow focus on completing concrete tasks so she can clear them from her never-ending to-do list.

In a collaboration revolution workplace, where the lines of authority are unclear and priorities become muddled, almost everyone worth their salt will tell you they're "always juggling." Often, they say it as if it's something to be proud of, proof that they are super busy with lots of "very important work."

And it's true: today you do need to work cross-functionally and handle a long and diverse list of responsibilities and projects. But that's precisely why juggling doesn't work. The busier you are and the heavier your workload, the less you can *afford* to be a juggler. Juggling is not a badge of honor. If you are juggling, it's just a matter of time before you drop some balls. In the end, you can only finish one thing at a time. So you need tools that help you execute one thing at a time. In other words, the goal is not to juggle until you somehow, eventually—almost by chance—complete a task or project. The goal is to finish what you start.

Which is just another way of saying "Get sh-t done."

Get Sh-t Done

One of my favorite senior executives, Mary Trout, who is an all-star MVP go-to person, says to most every new person she brings onto her team that one of her most important measures of success is simple: "Get sh-t done!" Everyone in her department knows the slogan well and many have the slogan emblazoned somewhere in their work area. One person has an 8.5" × 11" sheet of paper on his bulletin board with the initials "GSD" printed on it.

Done means done! Finished. Wrap it up. Complete one thing at a time. Then move on to the next thing.

Go-to people get sh-t done. You could say GSD is just another version of Sheryl Sandberg's much-repeated quote, "Done is better than perfect." So many people are so busy all the time, working so hard, but they do not GSD. At least, they don't get *enough* SD. Some people get halfway down the road to completing a task, and then they have second thoughts. Suddenly they change directions.

OK, that happens. Maybe there is a shift in circumstances, something totally unanticipated. After all, you have to be "change ready," flexible, adaptable, especially now when there's so much uncertainty. Change happens, and you have to deal with it.

But too often, people get partly into a project, and all at once they get cold feet. They lose faith in the direction they've taken. Maybe they are afraid to fail. Maybe they are afraid to succeed. Or maybe they just lose steam and fizzle out. For whatever reason, they just can't get all the way to the other side. And that ping or buzz or ring from one of their devices comes as a welcome diversion.

Or, even more common, people begin a task and then simply get distracted by the next buzz, ping, or ring. They convince themselves that they must respond—right now—or they'll miss something urgent. Or they worry they'll find themselves drowning later in the backlog of emails, texts, or voicemails they didn't answer right away. (See the sidebar "Practice Good Email Hygiene.") I'm not saying these aren't legitimate concerns. But they're often the reason that, day after day, jugglers just keep juggling—and don't finish what they start.

Don't Be a Juggler

Think about it: "juggling" is just a concept-and-a-half away from "multitasking." Multitasking, the wishful idea that a human being can do more than one thing at a time, has been largely debunked over the years by cognitive research. It turns out that what looks like multitasking at its best is actually "task shifting." The brain can shift, very rapidly, between one focus and another, even among several points of focus. So what's *actually* happening is not that the brain is focusing on several things at one time. Rather, it's simply shifting attention, over and over again, like switching channels—however rapidly—from one thing to the next. Like juggling.

A plethora of studies in brain science (see, for example, the work of Clifford Nass and Anthony Wagner at Stanford University), adding up to a growing body of research, demonstrates that juggling, multitasking, and other forms of "attention shifting" are highly inefficient. Simply, the brain works much faster and more accurately when attention is focused, for a stretch of

Practice Good Email Hygiene

One symbol of the collaboration revolution must surely be the little mail icon on our devices. All day long, it flashes the growing numbers of new emails puffing up our inboxes. But if you're responding to emails all day long (and into the night), you aren't likely to get sh-t done. Here's help:

- Send fewer and better messages (you'll get fewer back in return).

- Before sending a message, ask yourself if you shouldn't schedule a meeting with the person instead. Some things really are best communicated in person.

- Stop sending first drafts. Send first drafts to yourself.

- If you are messaging someone so you don't forget to tell them something, send the reminder to yourself instead.

- Only send copies to people who need to be cc'd, and do not reply all unless you need to reply to all.

time, on *one thing at a time*. The good news is that most people, according to the research, can focus on one thing in increments as long as thirty to forty-five minutes (at which point most brains need a little break).

That means you should set yourself up to work in focused increments without interruption—do-not-disturb zones in which you can execute and finish with tangible results, even if they are only chunks of a larger whole, one next step at a time. But most

- Use red flags and other indicators sparingly and with true purpose.

- Make subject lines smart; context is everything.

- Change subject lines on later emails if the subject changes.

- Make messages brief, simple, and orderly.

- Create a simple folder system for filing incoming and out-going electronic communication based on how you will use them later.

- Establish daily time blocks for reviewing and responding to electronic communication in batches rather than singly throughout the day. Manage people's expectations by telling them about this practice. That will give them an idea of when to expect responses from you.

people in the workplace don't do that. Most are always juggling, even though they think they are multitasking. They think they are doing more, but in truth they are doing less.

The classic examples are people who are always checking and responding to emails and texts during meetings. Maybe they really believe they're both responding to the emails *and* listening in the meeting. But they're actually not doing either one very well, certainly not with proper focus. "The meeting wasn't very important anyway," they might say. At which point I always want to ask, "How would you know? You weren't paying attention!"

These kinds of people often think meetings are usually a waste of time. So, I ask them, "What are you doing to make the meeting valuable?" Because, with their inattention, they often contribute to making the meeting longer and *less* valuable. These are the people who inevitably chime in toward the end to make a point or ask a question that was already addressed earlier in the meeting—when their eyes were on their phone.

Meetings can actually be very valuable. Here you have a bunch of people in a room for x amount of time. It's a huge investment of organizational resources—all that time and individual productive capacity channeled into one place and time. It is also a huge opportunity to share information, hear and respond spontaneously to each other, clarify priorities, make decisions, plan interdependent work such as handoffs from one person to another, troubleshoot, problem solve, check timelines, calibrate, and recalibrate. So, meetings are valuable, but only to the extent that people are focused enough to *make* them valuable.

And what about those emails and texts that jugglers are trying to address while sitting in the meeting? Aren't those communications valuable enough to warrant your full attention? I always ask jugglers, "How can you concentrate on reading, digesting, and responding optimally to those emails with all that meeting chatter in your ears?" They might say, "Oh, those emails weren't very important either." Again, how could they possibly know? There's no way they could be paying proper attention to those emails and texts. If they were, maybe they could make something important happen with them.

More to the point, who has time to do anything that's "not important"? Or to spend any time on an email or a meeting that you consider so unimportant that it doesn't require your focus?

If you want to be indispensable at work, you need to be known for executing on one important thing after another very well, very fast, all day long. That means purposefully *contributing to the value* of those things—be they meetings, emails, conversations, research, whatever—by giving them your full, focused attention.

Manage Your Time—Don't Let It Manage You

Nearly every self-help guru has observed that self-management and time management are the same thing. If you seize control of your time, you seize control of you. But how?

Whenever I'm working with a person like Juggler, who is clearly working very hard but struggling to get things done, I want to know, "What are you actually doing?" I'm not trying to catch them. I'm trying to help them catch up by gaining control of their time.

Think of every minute of your time as a unit of productive capacity. Your productivity is measured in your output per labor unit. It's not just how much time is allocated to one thing or another. The real measure is how much you get done in the time that is allocated.

Juggling means you are working in tiny increments of time, shifting back and forth between one thing and another, diminishing your speed and accuracy, and severely limiting the amount of focused execution time you have to block out for accomplishing high-priority items. The growing body of brain research shows that juggling, compared with focused execution, leads to increased error rates and diminished output. Focused execution, for longer increments of time (ideally thirty- to forty-five-minute increments), on the other hand, leads to decreased error rates and increased output.

So, don't juggle. Instead, set aside focused execution time. The trick is to find those gaps in your schedule when you can focus and *do*—and actually get things done. Here's how.

Keep a "Do" List—Not Just a To-Do List

Rafael works as a regulatory-affairs manager in an engineering firm. He has a near-superhuman workload, but he's one of the best people I've seen at finishing what he starts. He keeps a schedule and a to-do list. But he also keeps a "do" list. He showed me his system. He keeps two whiteboards mounted on the wall on either side of his desk. One whiteboard tracks Rafael's longer-term "Projects" (detailed in the left column) and his "Ongoing Responsibilities" for each project (detailed in the right column). That whiteboard was full when I saw it, and each item was color-coded to indicate its priority (e.g., red was his current priority number one).

The other whiteboard outlined Rafael's current day, and it also had two columns. The heading on the left column read, "Today," and it listed time slots in one-hour increments. The right-column heading read, simply, "Do."

I was surprised to see that this second whiteboard was mostly empty, which I found odd because Rafael was always so incredibly productive. Isn't "Today" supposed to be where all the action is?

The few things he'd listed on that whiteboard were in blocked-out time frames of thirty to sixty minutes. He had marked each time block with an arrow pointing to the "Do" column, where he'd written a brief notation (or a short list of notations).

Today		Do
6 a.m.		
7		
8		
9		
10	→	• paragraphs 3, 4 of safety filing SQF
11		
12 p.m.		
1		
2		
3		
4		
5	→	• write paragraphs 5, 6 of SQF
6	→	• review SQF and prepare to submit
7		
8		
9		
10		

You might think Rafael's system was a version of the common practice of using whiteboards to track goals and schedules and maintain to-do lists. But Rafael said no. "That's my 'do' list," he told me, "not my 'to-do' list." And, "That's not my schedule. Those are the only *gaps* in my schedule." He explained, "My schedule is back-to-back-to-back with meetings and conference calls. So I find and mark out those gaps every day, because those are my chance to focus"—and get sh-t done.

The two whiteboards are a great metaphor: while the longer-term list is relatively static, the daily list changes, not just every day, but all day long. Rafael said, "Those 'do' items almost never roll over from one day to the next. If it's on my 'do' list, I get it done and erase it."

So, don't just keep a to-do list. Start keeping a daily "do" list. And don't just keep a schedule. Identify your schedule gaps every day and use them for focused execution of the items on that "do" list.

Choose. Focus. Make It Count

Maybe you are thinking, "It's not always my choice what to do and when." You have too much to do and not enough time. You have a meeting. You have email. But you can only focus on one thing at a time. If you must choose, then choose. Meeting or email?

It's not what you are doing that makes a task, responsibility, or project important or not, but rather *how* you are doing it. Is your attention focused or scattered? Here's a simple rule: make everything you do count. If you must do it, then it's important enough to focus on. Get it done, very well, very fast. That's so simple, but most people don't do it. Even most busy, successful people in senior roles don't do it.

What about you? Are you making what you do count? One way to find out is by using a time log.

Keep a Time Log

The time log is a powerful tool that can help someone like Juggler, or you, gain control of your time. The time log will help you, if you do it in a truthful way. Be brutally honest with yourself about how you are really using your time—or how your time is using you.

Here's the very simple and powerful idea: every time you change your activity, you make a note of it and log the time.

If you are really going to keep a log, you have to commit to it. That means you have your time log with you and note every time you change activities. Do it for five hours. Try it for ten. Try doing it from 6 a.m. to 10 p.m. every day for three days, four days, five days. Do it for a while. You'll see what I mean. It's a powerful exercise: you will identify your biggest time wasters and, more important, the biggest schedule gaps in which you could get things done.

If you are a juggler, of course, this is going to be a very burdensome exercise. You'll have to make so many entries. But, that's one of the reasons it can be so powerful. It's a reality check.

Imagine Juggler's time log, including only my perspective, from the thirty-nine minutes I spent with her, as I described earlier:

2:58 p.m.   Finishing calculation, didn't finish it

2:59 p.m.   Answered phone call, ended it, will reschedule

3:01 p.m.   Meeting with consultant

3:27 p.m.   Incoming emails, texts, calls

3:31 p.m.   Better take the call

3:32 p.m.   Start looking at emails and texts, while on call

3:33 p.m.   Respond to text, still on call

3:35 p.m.   Respond to email, still on call

3:37 p.m.   End call, urgent situation to deal with . . . ended meeting with consultant prematurely, will reschedule

3:38 p.m.   Zoom in like the cavalry to deal with urgent situation

---

6:20 p.m.   Back at desk . . . trying to catch up

6:21 p.m.   ????

Have you ever tried using a time log? Try it. Then evaluate and learn how you actually use that precious limited resource—your time:

- Compare your time log to your list of top priorities. How does your time spending line up with your top priorities?

- What (or who) are your biggest time wasters? What lowest-priority activities are taking up your time? How can you eliminate them?

- Identify your biggest sources of interruption. What can you do to better manage those interruptions?

- Identify any unexpected emergencies or urgent matters that required your attention. What can you do to better anticipate and prevent those emergencies or urgencies going forward?

- Identify opportunities to increase your efficiency. What can you streamline? What shortcuts can you take? What detours can you avoid?

Now make your schedule for the coming week, taking into account what you've learned from keeping the time log. The golden goose you are looking for is *bigger chunks of time*. That's what you (and most people) are probably lacking. That's one of the things holding you back.

The time log will give you that brutal reality check about how you are using your time and then motivate you to take control of your time. In essence, you will take control of your time by slowing down. It's a two-part strategy:

1. Increase your smallest increments of time, the time spans spent on one activity before shifting activities. That way, you will start juggling more slowly, even if you are still juggling. The more you increase the time frames during which you are focused on one activity, the more you will get done.

2. Meanwhile, try to set aside more dedicated, bigger chunks of time (thirty to forty-five minutes) for focused execution on top priorities. The more dedicated time chunks you set aside, the more you will get done.

It's simple: slow down the juggling. Increase your focused execution time. (Of course, it's likely that some people will interrupt your focused execution time. See the sidebar "Dealing with Interruptions" for some tips.)

Dealing with Interruptions

No matter how many time chunks you manage to set aside, you are still going to get interrupted. What do you do?

One of the most relentless (some might say ruthless) time chunkers I know, an incredibly productive individual and a classic go-to person, taught me a very simple rule: "If the building is on fire, then interrupt me. Otherwise, almost anything can wait for forty-five minutes."

People will still interrupt you. The more people interrupt you, the more you need to channel their interruptions into regular one-on-one structured dialogues, as discussed in chapter 3. Teach people what to expect from you: "If the building is on fire, then interrupt me. But otherwise, let's schedule some time."

This idea might irritate you. Maybe you're the kind of person who likes telling colleagues, "My door is always open." The trouble is, if you want to get sh-t done, your door can't always be open.

The good news is that structured dialogue is always better and more productive than random, ad hoc communication—

Now, Take Control of Your Time

The goal is to start doing everything in larger increments of time and dedicating more and more big chunks to your most important activities.

for everyone involved. And that strategy allows you to enjoy more thirty- to forty-five-minute chunks when you can work straight through, without interruption. The more chunks you have, the more you will get done and the more time you will create for yourself and others who want your attention.

Eventually, you will get to the point that the relentless time chunker I described above reached. He told me, "I set aside a chunk of time late in the day to sort through my interruptions and then respond to them. By late in the day, usually a good share of these interruptions becomes irrelevant. They go away on their own. Overtaken by events. Most of the rest, I send a note and schedule a time. That's another dedicated time chunk."

The problem with interruptions is that, if you deal with them as they come in, you have no way to rank them in order of priority. You take them as they come, regardless of how important they may be.

When you take control of your time and dedicate time chunks, you can allocate your time in order of priority.

So, do you know what your most important activities are right now? You will if you are going vertical and are aligned up and down your chain of command. What would your boss say were your most important activities? What would your boss's boss say? What about your direct reports—do they know what they should be devoting their own time chunks to?

Are you aligning with your sideways and diagonal working partners? What are their priorities? Where do those square with those of your chain of command?

What are your own priorities? Set priorities and revisit them regularly. What are your most important tasks, responsibilities, and projects? What is the most important right now at work? Why? Are you sure? What is number two? Number three? Do you have time for any more than three right now? How are you allocating your time among your top three priorities right now?

It's OK if you have five or ten or fifteen priorities. But you cannot, absolutely cannot, have more than three *right now*. What is right now for you? Today? Tomorrow? This week? Next week? Three weeks from now is a vision. It is not here yet. What are you going to do right now? Answering that question is how you gain control of your time right now.

If you have limited time and too much to do, then you need to set priorities—an order of precedence or preference for your tasks—so that you control what gets done first, second, and third. Today, what's going to be first, second, and third? Nothing else matters today.

That means, every week, every day, plan every step of your work. Break big projects into manageable tasks, estimate accurately how long they will each take to complete, and set a timetable based on those realistic estimates. Sure, you will still have to juggle some. But remember, you are trying to quit.

OK, here's the twist. If you are going to start getting more and more done, then you must expand your units of productive capacity and increase the number of increments in your day when you can set aside focused execution time. At the same time, you must *break your work* into smaller and smaller chunks.

How small? That depends. As small as it takes to keep you moving from one concrete action to the next, from one next step to another, so you can finish what you start. Every concrete action can be broken down into smaller and smaller components, and each small component itself can be broken down into still smaller components.

Whenever I'm working with anybody, at any level, who is getting bogged down, working like crazy, but somehow not getting enough done, I always do the same thing: I help them break each concrete action into smaller chunks. Smaller and smaller chunks. Smaller and smaller. Until, if necessary, I am saying, "Send a message from your brain to your right index finger. Type the *m* key. Now send a message from your brain to your left index finger. Type the *r* key." And so on.

It might sound crazy or extreme, but try it. Any time you get bogged down, break every task into its smaller and smaller components, and then start tackling them one small chunk at a time. You'll see it works. You will start moving forward.

Bigger chunks of *time*. Smaller chunks of *work*. That's the ticket.

Bite-Size Chunks of Work

There are a million metaphors for breaking bigger tasks into smaller pieces—projects broken into intermediate goals; intermediate goals into smaller goals; specific lists of concrete actions in between each of the smaller goals.

This is the metaphor I prefer: How do you eat an elephant? One bite at a time. I think of every concrete action as a bite-size chunk of an elephant. Here's why that's my preferred metaphor:

you have to chew and swallow one bite of the elephant before you can take the next bite. So, don't stuff your mouth with elephant. Carve up everything into bite-size chunks. Then bite, chew, swallow. Look around: do you need to tune in to an interruption? Let's hope not. Bite, chew, swallow.

You don't have to eat the whole elephant in one sitting. Set aside chunks of time every day—without interruptions—for focused execution, ideally thirty- to forty-five-minute time blocks. How many bite-size chunks can you eat at one sitting?

Everybody is different. You need to figure out *your* optimal time chunk for focusing and *your* optimal bite size. Maybe you'll have different time chunks for different sorts of bites. Whatever it is, start there.

Do a time-motion study on your own work. For any task, responsibility, or project you are analyzing, you'll have to do a separate time-motion study. This technique may appeal more to the obsessive-compulsive variety of overachievers, like one tax preparer I interviewed in an accounting firm who prided herself on moving through document lines swiftly and with precision; or the very artistic but also notably driven metal fabricator who showed me how he "keeps score" for himself all day long on the rate of his pieces completed to specs. There's also the extroverted salesperson who counts every outgoing call, message left, call duration, hit rate on all the message points per call, and, of course, leads generated, and ultimately, completed sales. Why those measures? "That's how we get paid, right? It's that simple."

It doesn't matter what you do, if you want to do it faster and better, measure yourself in more-granular terms and use those measures to drive your performance. It's a way of coaching yourself. If you want to run faster, you time your runs and maybe start timing each segment. If you want to do more push-ups, you count your push-ups. If you want to make sure to do good push-ups, you do them in front of the mirror and then be honest with yourself about your form.

Start by breaking each task into its component steps or checklist. Then break each step into a series of concrete actions:

- Bite

- Chew

- Swallow

Time each step within each task; time each concrete action within each step. How long does each task take? Each step within each task? Each concrete action within each step? That will tell you how much time the whole task takes.

How long do you *think* it should take? Create a time budget for every task, every step, every concrete action.

Take it to the next level. Use your time-motion budgets to help you keep score for yourself going forward.

- If you are behind schedule, do a micro-gap analysis. Identify the micro-gaps between the time budget you made and your actual time step by step, concrete action by concrete action. In these micro-gaps lie the potential opportunities to speed up.

- If you want to speed up, choose one concrete action at a time to accelerate and then work on speeding them up by closing the micro-gaps one by one. By going one concrete action at a time, you will minimize the chances of increased mistakes in the effort to speed up.

- Are you sure you are doing each concrete step correctly? Are you doing any unnecessary actions or steps that might slow you down? Are you encountering any recurring obstacles that you can remove?

Start with High-Leverage Time Investments

What if you can only set aside one chunk of time—thirty to forty-five minutes? Or one per week? Or one per day? If you can only set aside one chunk, how should you spend it? You should spend it on your top priority, of course. But what should that be?

Do you remember, when you were young, kids liked to ask each other a trick riddle? "If you could have any wish granted, but you have only one wish, what would you wish for?" The optimal answer, by some standards, was, "More wishes." That's the same answer to the question: "If you have just one chunk of dedicated time, what should your top priority be?" My answer: creating more chunks of dedicated time. How? By spending your dedicated time chunks doing what I call "high-leverage" activities. That is time you spend preventing a problem (fire prevention), putting in motion a necessary step that must precede a later step in a sequential process (preheating the oven before you can start baking), or activating someone or something else's productive capacity (effectively delegating a task or, let's say, programming the robot).

High-leverage time invested will save you more time later. Think of the steps laid out in the preceding chapters. They are all examples of super high-leverage time investments:

- Do the right things in the right order for the right reasons, one moment at a time, to add value and serve others. The purpose is to make things better for everybody in the long term and build up your real influence.

- Align your communication—up, down, sideways, and diagonal—through structured dialogue with anybody you are working with for any period of time.

- Do your due diligence—tuning in to every ask, considering the no gates, and turning every yes into a plan.

- Work smart—professionalizing everything you do with best practices, repeatable solutions, and job aids; specializing in whatever you do best; and expanding your repertoire of specialties.

Dedicating time blocks in your day to focused execution so you can start and finish one thing at a time on your "do" list is not just a high-leverage time investment, it is a meta-high-leverage time investment.

When you start getting serious about taking control of your time, it may be difficult at first. That's because you will still be in the habit of juggling, and you'll still have plenty of fires to fight. You don't want to drop any balls. You can't let the building burn down. So, you can't just take control of all of your time all at once. You might have to get up earlier in the morning for a while in order to set aside those high-leverage chunks and start making more time for yourself.

Make the transition. Do it one meta-high-leverage chunk at a time. The more high-leverage time you set aside for yourself, the more time you are going to save for yourself in the future, creating more and more schedule gaps in which you can get things done.

There are 168 hours in a week. Nobody is creating any more hours. Actually, yes, you can. High-leverage time chunks are like a factory for manufacturing more time. That's where you should be working, as much as possible.

What if you just started with one dedicated high-leverage time chunk per day? In your schedule, set aside that time chunk now for tomorrow. Just thirty to forty-five minutes. While you're at it, set aside a chunk for every day this week. Then *use* those chunks. You'll be amazed at the impact. The more time chunks you create, the more time chunks you will create.

Remember: GSD

Some people say, "It's better to take the journey than to arrive at the destination." Yes, in life. But, no, not at work. At work, you have to GSD. Done is better than perfect. Move on to the next thing. Finish what you start. Then keep getting better and better at working together. It's all about lifting other people up and getting lifted up by other people. Focus your relationship building on the work, and the work will go better. Plan the next collaboration by looking around the corner together. The next chapter will show you how.

CHAPTER SUMMARY

- Don't be a juggler.

  - If you are juggling, it's just a matter of time before you drop some balls.

- Get sh-t done.

  - You can only finish one thing at a time.

- Find the gaps in your schedule.

  - Your schedule gaps are uncommitted chunks of time.

- Turn your schedule gaps into do-not-disturb zones.

  - Execute and finish tangible results, even if they are only chunks of a larger whole, one next step at a time.

- Make smaller and smaller chunks of work.

  - Chew and swallow one bite of the elephant before you can take the next bite. You don't have to eat the whole elephant in one sitting.

- Start keeping a daily "do" list.

  - What are you going to *do* today, in those gaps—that do-not-disturb zone? Finish it, and erase it? Bite, chew, swallow.

- Start with high-leverage time.

  - This is the time you spend preventing a problem, putting in motion a necessary step that must precede a later step in a sequential process, or activating someone or something else's productive capacity.

7

Keep Getting Better and Better at Working Together

We all know that "building relationships is critical to success" any time, but especially so in today's workplace. "People are our number-one asset!" The problem is that such truisms lead a lot of would-be go-to people in the wrong direction when trying to tap the power of relationships at work. First, there are those who play workplace politics:

- *The blamer.* Blamers always can (and usually do) tell you (and lots of others) all of the things that other people do wrong (or not quite right) that lead to suboptimal results.

Shane, a retail sales whiz at a makeup counter in a major department store, specializes in makeovers—and turning makeovers into sales. Not only does he make a point of keeping score of his own successes, he is also ready to tell anybody who will listen exactly why any sale he misses is somebody else's fault. It might be the buyers who sometimes fail to keep up inventory on his best-selling products or that salesperson who "scares away" his customers before he gets to them, or the assistant managers who sometimes don't let him give a customer the discount he "needs" to give. The blamer makes darn sure that his boss (and everyone else) knows whom to blame, but, of course, it's never Shane.

The irony is that Shane's complaints potentially reveal very important information about problems in his department. But pointing fingers at others is no way to drive continuous improvement.

- *The lobbyist.* Lobbyists are always ready to tell anybody who will listen about what they want (or need): the next big project, a new location, a different schedule, training, or of course, the next raise or promotion. And they lobby not just for themselves but also for others. Maggie, a manufacturing manager, is always there to tell her boss why she and her team should get credit for anything and everything, and why they need more resources—people, money, time—if they are going to keep up with the production schedule. Maggie also spends a lot of time trying to impress big shots, not just her boss, but also her boss's boss, and her boss's boss's boss. Of course, Maggie manages to do her share of blaming others in one breath, even as she lobbies for something she wants in the next breath—especially if she's trying to deflect attention from an error made by her team.

Like the blamer, the lobbyist may actually have some good reasons for bringing certain information to the table. But if you are always lobbying—"more for me, more for us"—you begin to lack credibility, and the underlying problems may well remain unresolved.

Both the blamer and the lobbyist are classic types who try to use *politics* to gain relationship power on the job. The blamer does that by tearing down other people, usually behind their backs. The lobbyist does that by advocating for her (and others') wants and needs, often by trading favors or making threats, however veiled those threats might be. Or sometimes you'll see lobbyists trying to build relationships by ingratiating themselves—through flattery or favors—with people who have authority and influence.

Maybe even more common than playing politics, many would-be go-to people seek to build relationship power at work by relying on *personal rapport*:

- *Mr. Personality.* This person at work tries to build relatively shallow personal rapport. I remember Barney, a shipping and receiving manager, who knew everybody in the entire headquarters. If you shipped or received anything, Barney knew your name. Every morning, he'd make a big lap—into the cafeteria, down the hallways, walking by everybody's cubicle—saying hello by name. Occasionally, Barney would stop and shoot the breeze about this or that TV show, his doctor's visit, his child's activities. Barney was also always available to have coffee or step outside for another cigarette. He was the kind of guy who participated in everybody else's break. The problem was, he never seemed to have time to improve his work—such as making a better plan for keeping the supply chain moving through his shipping bays. Whenever something went wrong in the process, though, suddenly Barney got very serious, and those conversations didn't go well. Despite all that personal rapport Barney was always building, it did nothing to make the work go better. And when the work got problematic, all that rapport went right out the window.

- *Ms. Best Friend.* This person really wants to go deep with personal rapport building. Now, don't get me wrong. I realize that sometimes you actually are best friends with a coworker, or you work with a spouse, sibling, or cousin. That has its own set of complications to manage. What I'm talking about here is the person who tries to become best friends at work (lunch or maybe drinks after work) or else *real* best friends (weekend get-togethers with each other's families). I remember Frida, who was definitely the best-friend type, stopping by everybody's desk to show them pictures of her kids, but she didn't have kids. They were actually pictures of another colleague's kids, which she had conveniently on her person. Of course, if you have deep friendships at work, so be it. But there are a number of issues here: those personal affinities don't help you plan the work so it goes better. And when the work goes badly, sometimes it is very hard for a best friend like Frida to hold people accountable or take corrective action. And people like Frida sometimes end up forming workplace cliques, based on personal affinities, that exclude other coworkers.

Both Mr. Personality and Ms. Best Friend work very hard at relationship building. Sometimes it seems that's *too much* of what they do. The problem is that Mr. Personality's relationships are based on paper-thin connections—all style, no substance. And Ms. Best Friend is so busy going deep that she may build her workplace loyalties for plenty of non-work-related reasons and miss out on other potentially valuable working relationships in the process. And all that socializing can be a big distraction. (See the sidebar "The Research on BFFs at Work.")

But aren't all these characters—the people who seek to leverage personal rapport or office politics at work—simply doing what we've all been told to do to survive today? Haven't we all learned that relationship building is how we get along and get things done in the collaboration revolution?

The Trouble with Relationship Building

If you're working in an organization now, you've been well tutored in two of the truest truisms of the collaboration revolution:

"People are our number-one asset!"

"Building relationships is critical to your success!"

The problem is that, like the blamer, the lobbyist, Mr. Personality, and Ms. Best Friend, too many would-be go-to people emphasize the wrong aspects of relationship building. They conflate

The Research on BFFs at Work

When I say "build the relationship," I'm not talking about finding best friends at work. Our research shows that having best friends at work—especially if that person is your boss or direct report—will likely complicate your working relationship. That's another whole can of worms.

I'm also not talking about building work relationships by engaging in nonwork socializing. Our research shows the pros and cons of socializing with colleagues outside of work to build personal rapport. If you want to have drinks and food and shoot darts or chat with your colleagues, outside of work, that's your business. But that's a whole other thing too.

What I mean when I say, "Take the time to build the relationship in between work transactions" is to build up the *working* part of your relationships with more and more people—up, down, sideways, and diagonal. These people can become your best internal customers. They also can become your go-to people, which allows you to become *their* best internal customer.

relationship power with politics, popularity, or even friendship. That's always a big mistake. Those aspects of relationships have their place, but they don't do enough to get the work done better and faster.

And they often make things worse. Despite all the time and energy dedicated to relationships, there is simply not enough structured communication to ensure alignment, due diligence, planning, and execution. That means the *same things* go wrong with the work as last time, and once again, there's no real systematic follow-up after the fact to fine-tune the process of working together.

Whenever the work goes wrong, regardless of the personal rapport and politics, the pressure on those relationships increases exponentially. That's when people start complaining about each other, blaming, and finger-pointing, which undermines the relationships rather than making them stronger. Whatever personal rapport and politics you have built up goes right out the window. Yes, good rapport with one's colleagues is a must, and political dynamics are necessary. Also there is critical data to be found in blaming, complaining, and finger-pointing.

How can you take the best aspects of politicking and building personal rapport to craft the kinds of solid relationships you seek to make yourself indispensable at work? First, you can foster *authentic rapport* with people at work by talking about what you actually have in common and need to stay focused on: the work you do together. That rapport will help make the work go better, and it won't disappear when the work goes wrong.

Note how different that description is from how Mr. Personality and Ms. Best Friend try to build rapport. And remember Connie, the brownie baker in chapter 2? She tried to influence and build rapport with Andrew in shipping by being a friend and dropping off baked goods whenever she had a shipment coming through. That made Andrew uncomfortable. He decided to build authentic rapport with Connie by working with her more closely. He helped her understand the steps necessary to navigate inspections so there wouldn't be any problems with her shipments.

Second, you can build *enduring political power* at work by being a reliable public servant in relation to the mission, the chain of command, and your colleagues. Again, note how different that description sounds from the way the blamer and the lobbyist do things. Remember Lisa Wolf, the ER nurse, also in chapter 2? Her political power and real authority at work came from her attitude of *service*. Everyone around her knew that what she said mattered, because she cared about the department's mission and was aligned in every direction. In addition, everyone wanted Lisa to have even more power because Lisa's power helped them get their needs met.

Just like Lisa and Andrew, you have to be able to channel political power and rapport building in the right direction—at getting better and better at working together. Taken alone, personal rapport and politics are not the same thing as *systematic, continuous improvement* of your day-to-day working interactions.

In today's workplace, we seek to practice ongoing, continuous improvement in nearly every area and aspect of the organization. We also need to apply those practices in an ongoing, continuous way to improve our *working relationships*—up, down, sideways, and diagonal.

The key to continuous improvement is capturing the lessons to be learned when things go wrong—instead of finger-pointing. But it also means capturing lessons when things go *right* and celebrating them. Because to get better at working together, you also have to acknowledge and understand your successes so you can duplicate and improve on them.

What could be more important than continuously improving our management of our number-one asset?

Continuous Improvement

In every workplace I visit, I hear plenty of praise and admiration among people for their coworkers:

"This person is great."

I also hear people complain every day—about other people or teams or entire departments:

"I wouldn't want to work with that person again."

"If I'm going to work with that person again, I'd definitely do some things differently."

This all makes tons of sense. The funny thing is how much all of those comments actually contain such very important information. Those opinions, and the details below the surface, hold the keys to improving our relationships.

Because, once you've completed a piece of the puzzle, or even an entire project, or gotten the product out the door with bells, whistles, and a bow on top, it's still not done—or at least, you shouldn't be done. That's where a whole new kind of magic happens, after the work itself is done. The magic that drives continuous improvement happens when you take one more step: *a systematic postwork follow-up process.* The basic question you want to answer is: What can we do better together to improve our process, results, and working relationship? Taking this critical step, postwork debriefing, doesn't come naturally in most organizations. Not enough companies build in postwork follow-up review and relationship building to their checklists and process steps. Most are more concerned with moving on to the next project, as quickly as possible. And I understand why. People tend to fall into a routine, especially when working with the same people over and over. They take for granted that they'll always work together, more or less well, and they move on to the next project.

Or at the other end of the spectrum are those periodic, occasional, or even out-of-the-blue, working relationships. We assume that when we finish the interaction or transaction, it is over and done, a one-off. We don't stop and think about the next time we might find ourselves working together again.

Both ends of the spectrum are missed opportunities for continuous improvement in your working relationships.

With people you always work with, there's always room to improve, whether you're aware of it or not. You'll never find out if you don't take the final step of engaging in a postwork process.

And what about the one-offs, those people you never normally work with except on this one project? Don't kid yourself: there's likely to be a next time. Why not make the next time even better than this time?

You will need some discipline and maybe some insistence to include a postwork process after the work itself is done. That means that after every working interaction or transaction, you follow up and build the relationship before the next interaction or transaction.

What It Takes to Get Better and Better

The follow-up is a way for a go-to person to apply the process of regular continuous improvement directly to the working part of working relationships. That means you (1) celebrate success and thank people for their contributions, (2) examine and fine-tune your modus operandi for working together, and (3) try to plan for next time.

Step One: Make a Great "Thank You"
One of Your Signatures

People at all levels in the workplace tell me that "we don't stop often enough to acknowledge what we've done and celebrate some of our successes." Celebration and acknowledgment are the first step in the continuous improvement process because, without them, people start feeling beaten down and disheartened. They begin to wonder what the point is and even question why they try so hard when no one seems to even notice their work.

That's a problem, because it's really quite amazing how much people accomplish for each other at work. While lots of people find plenty of time to blame and complain when things go wrong, most do not take enough time to stop and appreciate each other when things go right.

One reason is that even major initiatives in organizations rarely have a tidy ending that can be celebrated. Most initiatives have ongoing clean-up and next stages. They are, more or less, never-ending. But it's still important to pause and acknowledge what's been accomplished and to thank all the players. If the project is never-ending, stop along the way to celebrate and thank people—*before* you continue on to the next stages.

Celebration can come in many forms. Maybe when your team completes phase one of a major initiative, there's some kind of recognition—at least from management—of the people who worked on it. Maybe there is an employee of the month or a quarterly meeting where people receive special recognition. Or maybe there's simply a pizza party and you exchange high fives with others on the team.

The real go-to person makes sure to pause, celebrate, and thank people for what's been accomplished. In the organizations I've worked with, I've seen so many official and unofficial ways to acknowledge people for the work they've done.

Official recognition. Some organizations are better at this than others. Sales organizations do a great job measuring and awarding specific goals, like dollar targets. So they are good models of high recognition and thanks. Exceed your numbers in a sales role and people will notice: usually salespeople are ranked by the numbers, and top sales are recognized with certificates, president's club membership, wristwatches, or attendance at incentive vacation trips, and always money.

But there is always so much important performance that cannot be easily measured, but nonetheless deserves official recognition and thanks. Salespeople cannot always control their top line or their bottom line; there are factors outside their control. But it's still so important for salespeople to ask the right questions, use the right messages, and even if the sale isn't made today or this week, cultivate customer relationships and nurture the sale for the long term.

How do you create a culture of recognition and celebration around that sort of valuable but hard-to-measure behavior? Of course, managers need to be aware of those dimensions of performance, ask salespeople to track their own performance, listen to random samples of calls, and recognize success in these areas despite the fact they are hard to measure.

That's what's done in the most effective sales organizations I've observed. In one organization in particular, every week, there's a theme, key questions, or messages it is pushing salespeople to use on the phone. Everybody records all of their calls, and there is always someone to keep score on how well they do with those questions in their calls. Meanwhile, coworkers are encouraged (in between their own incoming calls) to listen in on their colleagues' calls and to learn from each other. Along the way, coworkers are empowered to hand out "great question!" and "on message!" tags to each other. People proudly display their tags and also give them to others, repurposing the tags they've been given. It is a simple form of peer recognition that has become central to that organization's sales culture.

The US armed forces are also great at official recognition. There are medals awarded and promotions made to higher ranks, all based largely on clear measurable criteria. But you also will find in every branch of the military what are called "challenge coins" or "command coins," a wonderful form of thanks and acknowledgment that does not require an Act of Congress or approval up the chain of command. Rather, command-level leaders are issued a certain number of specially designed coins, personalized to the commander, that the leaders can then hand out to whomever they choose for just about any reason. They're a form of instant and personal, often private, acknowledgment and thanks. Service people prize these challenge coins, usually saving them forever and often displaying the coins they're especially proud to have received.

Over the years, I've received many of these coins myself from officials of the US armed forces following a successful brief on our research to a group of military leaders or following a speech or seminar. I count them among my most prized possessions. It is a good illustration of the flexible way the coins are used. After all, I've never had the honor of wearing the uniform of any branch of service, and yet commanders have seen fit to recognize and reward my contributions—in that moment and in ways that I still value, decades later, far more than the fees I was paid at the time.

These examples of official recognition and thanks—from the organization itself or from individuals leading from wherever they are—*matter*. People really appreciate it. And most organizations don't do enough of it. So, wherever you are, do whatever is in your power to optimize these official channels of recognition and thanks.

Unofficial recognition. Again, we can look to the military, which is replete with opportunities for relatively informal recognition and thanks. These range from exempting a well-performing new recruit from "drop and do push-ups" or cleaning the latrine, to awarding long-term service people who have good records with special assignments, training, or informal peer leadership opportunities.

Those are examples of unofficial rewards that people with rank can grant. But what if you don't have that kind of rank, whether you're in the military or some other organization? You still want to find ways to acknowledge the people with whom you work regularly. They are doing important work, accomplishing a lot for you or simply helping you out on a regular basis.

Even if you lack the authority to grant people time off or give them a special assignment, there is a way you can acknowledge their contributions. Get in the habit of saying "thank you." Did I really say that? Yes, I did. "Thank you," like "please," is as old as the hills. But like "please," I'm afraid "thank you" has gone out of fashion. When we do say it, too often it's in a perfunctory way.

A meaningful thank-you can be especially valuable in sideways and diagonal relationships. Too often, we get in the habit of feeling too much frustration with each other, usually because neither side understands the challenges the other faces.

But just as complaining, blaming, and finger-pointing leave people with a bad feeling, thank-you leaves people with a good feeling. Appreciation yields the inverse of the "disdain breeds disdain" rule. If you treat somebody with disdain, of course, you give that person a psychological incentive to diminish your opinion and to want you to be less powerful. Inversely, if you demonstrate understanding and appreciation of someone's contribution, you create a psychological incentive in the individual to give greater weight to your opinion. And that person will want to strengthen the weight of your opinion in the eyes of others. Appreciation and gratitude breed appreciation and gratitude.

As great as saying "thank you" can be, however, whenever you can, go beyond that. Do more than simply saying "thank you." One of the most thoughtful and appreciative individuals I've ever met prides himself on a very simple but surprisingly powerful thank-you technique. He calls it "my supersonic recognition thank-you." He says:

I write a letter to that person, detailing exactly what they've done. It's almost like an award citation, with bullet points outlining everything. Then I send them the letter, but I also copy everyone I can possibly think of, including their boss, their boss's boss, my boss, my boss's boss. I copy it to the company newsletter and the person's HR file. I share it with anyone I can. I send it by email, but I also print it out for the person I'm thanking, with all the cc's listed. So the individual can see I'm trying to shine a bright light of recognition on them. I've had quite a few people put those letters on their bulletin boards or even frame them.

That's an example of what one leader does, but you don't have to be a leader or a boss to write a supersonic recognition thank-you. You, too, can deputize yourself and turn your thank-you into a public commendation. Or figure out your own approach.

Make a great thank-you one of your signatures, like your own challenge coin. It costs you nothing, and it breeds a lot of good-will at work and in the world. (See the sidebar "Getting Really Good at Gratitude.")

People sometimes tell me, "But I interact with so many people every day. It's hard to even notice when someone does something well, much less to make time to thank them for it." It's true. Life and work often seem to move at warp speed. How can we pause and do justice to acknowledging anything, much less every deserving instance?

One way is to keep a daily "gratitude list." People who practice listing, in the morning or before bed, what and whom they're grateful for report a remarkable thing. Someone they hadn't

Getting Really Good at Gratitude

Tune in to being truly thankful and then put it out there:

1. Pay attention to other people. Be outward focused and mindful of the other people in your interactions.

2. Register what the other people are doing to add value in those interactions or transactions.

3. Take a moment to appreciate their effort, their technique, their attitude, their contributions; what they are doing well.

4. Choose one thing you especially appreciate about one person and describe to yourself what you appreciate and why.

5. At the right time, articulate to that person exactly what you appreciate and why.

6. Say "thank you!"

The most powerful forms of thank-you specifically describe the individuals' efforts and the value or impact of those efforts. If you want to take it to the next level, put your thank-you in writing. Or say it publicly in a group setting, if appropriate.

really noticed consciously—at work or in their daily lives—often pops up on the list. Maybe the postal carrier is always careful to place packages out of sight from the street when you're not home. Or a colleague always volunteers to take notes in a meeting. Those people deserve a thank-you. Don't forget to do that, in whatever form you choose.

One of the biggest frustrations in today's workplace is dealing with so many people we have little ability to "hold accountable" because we don't have enough authority to punish and reward people. Expressing gratitude, saying thank you, is a reward you can give out without any official authority whatsoever.

A bonus effect is that when you go out of your way to demonstrate appreciation for someone's valuable contribution, you make them want to work with you again and do a great job for you. It's what Dale Carnegie describes in his classic *How to Win Friends and Influence People*: "Give somebody a great reputation to live up to." And help create more go-to people in the process.

Step Two: Examine and Fine-Tune Your Modus Operandi

If you took all the complaining, blaming, and finger-pointing in the workplace and channeled it into continuous improvement, imagine how much better everybody would work together. Even in the most successful work interactions or transactions, where you can think of lots of things that went right, there are usually some things that could have gone better.

Every time you think, "I wish I had known *xyz*" or "Next time we should do *abc*," those are opportunities to get better. Don't miss them. Write them down, talk them through, and use the insights to improve.

That's what go-to people do. They get in the habit of doing some form of an after-action review following every significant action or project. In working relationships, such a practice is the heart of continuous improvement.

Make the after-action review your standard operating procedure. Do a structured analysis and debrief of what happened, why it happened, what went right, what went wrong, and how it can be done better going forward:

How did that sales call go?

Did I jump into the conversation too soon?

Did I have a chance to ask the right questions?

Did I have a chance to provide the right messages?

Maybe I should have jumped into the conversation at that point?

How can we work together better on this next time?

Originally developed by the US Army, the after-action review soon spread widely among military and intelligence organizations. Today, more and more private-sector organizations rely on it, especially those grounded in continuous improvement practices.

After-action reviews can be formal or informal. Perhaps you have been part of a more formal post-project postmortem or lessons-learned session, where a whole project team may go over systems, practices, competencies, and improvements that can be made to the process, to the whole group dynamic, and to the performance of individual participants.

Or maybe you've been part of less formal discussions in the middle of a project or afterward about how to improve together as a team or as individuals. In organizations where after-action reviews are a big part of the culture, people will often hold quick informal after-action reviews even after minor actions.

For example, if a team is training on a particular maneuver or for a particular mission, it may go through the same scenario or exercise multiple times, stopping for a quick after-action review in between each exercise to keep fine-tuning how the team is working together, with a particular focus on how each individual is playing a particular role in the exercise. In that way, the team uses quick, informal after-action reviews to accelerate the efficacy of training for a maneuver or mission.

Think of a sports team practicing a particular play, over and over, stopping briefly throughout practice to review, and steadily improving in each successive drill how the members are executing the play. Then, in the middle of the game, they make the play. They use their after-action review habits on the field to quickly discuss how it went and how they can make it even better next time.

After-action reviews can focus on how a process runs or how a whole group dynamic can function better. Or they can be tightly focused on the actions of individual participants, who are expected to answer questions such as:

- What were the intended results of my decisions and actions versus the actual results?

- What decisions and actions did I take?

- What better decisions and better actions could I have taken?

If you are engaging in a recurring process for a standing team, you might periodically conduct a stop, continue, start–style after-action review for the team and/or for each individual. That's a classic continuous improvement technique used in innovation and manufacturing processes, among other things. The basic questions used in such reviews are:

- What needs to stop?

- What should continue?

- What needs to start?

Imagine the impact those kinds of reviews have on the work in progress. Drive those reviews at the end of every step and at the finish of the project to inform the next project.

Make after-action reviews a habit. Even if your organization doesn't do it, your manager doesn't do it, and nobody else on your team does it, you should start a review on your own. Purposeful self-evaluation is critical to self-improvement. And learning to improve from how you handled past interactions and projects is the ultimate way to make yourself indispensable.

The review doesn't have to be long and involved. It can be quick. When things go wrong, instead of pointing fingers, examine the five *W*s and the *H*: *How did it happen, and who did what, why, where, and when?*

Review when things go right, too. If you can sell your colleague or team on the idea, it doesn't have to be a long conversation. It could be a quick huddle, using the following questions as your guide:

- What happened?

- Why did it happen?

- What went right?

- What went wrong?

- How could it go better next time?

For a deeper dive, ask:

- What were the intended results?

- What were the actual results?

- What decisions were made and actions taken?

- What better decisions could have been made and actions taken?

- Might there have been different results?

Clearly, with any colleague with whom you do regular after-action reviews, you'll find yourself working better and better. You will learn more and more about where they are coming from and where they are going. You will learn not just about how to work better with them, but how to work better with others similarly situated to that colleague. With that kind of ongoing self-evaluation in dialogue with others, you'll almost surely learn plenty, too, about how you can work better in so many ways.

When you get into this habit, especially with those you work with regularly, you build an expectation of, and mutual commitment to, continuously improving together. Such a discipline sends a powerful message of your commitment, service orientation, and positive attitude. The message of this practice is, "Together we're going to keep getting better at working together." It makes people want to keep going to you over and over again.

Step Three: Plan Ahead—at Least around the Corner

Let's assume that, after reading and following at least some of the advice in these pages, more people will more likely *want* to work with you again.

The final step of continuous improvement in your working relationships is to look around the corner for future opportunities to collaborate and to anticipate the next time you might have a chance to be of service to each other. But what about the people you're sure you *never* want to work with again? Whatever you may want, you may leave them wanting more from you. Don't stint on your thank-you or the after-action review. Still, that doesn't mean you will be available the next time they want to work with you.

One way to be less available to work with people you do not want to work with is to be already so engaged in working with people you do want to work with. So, plan ahead. End every work interaction or transaction by looking around the corner for the next opportunity to be of service to each other.

Even if you don't want to work together again, you should look around the corner together before parting ways. If you really truly want to avoid working with this person again, then it's good to know in advance when they might be coming for you next. Generally, of course, you want to try to stay on good terms with everybody. You never know when a working relationship is going to return, even if it didn't go very well this time.

The main goal of looking around the corner after every work interaction is to proactively fill up your schedule, working with those people you really do want to work with as much as possible. They are your preferred customers, the people with whom you've managed to do good work and work well together. You know how to stay in dialogue and in alignment; you make good decisions together, get a lot of work done very well very fast together, follow good best practices and use repeatable solutions together, and make each other feel appreciated and continuously improve your working relationship. You want to plan ahead so you can reserve as much time as possible for those people, and they can reserve time for you.

An Upward Spiral in the Making

As you keep getting better at working together with more people, you'll be a go-to person for more and more preferred customers. And you'll be a preferred customer for more go-to people. The goal is not to build a circle of friends at work or a professional clique that somehow excludes others. The goal is to have more preferred customers, the people you really know how to serve. And the goal is also to build up more go-to people, the people who really know how to serve you. Sure, these often turn out to be the same people. But it's not a popularity contest. It's not a quid pro quo.

You can never have too many go-to people, and you can never have too many preferred customers. It's an upward spiral of people getting better and better at working together. I call it go-to-ism, or the art of being indispensable at work. Turn to the last chapter to discover how to build an upward spiral of real influence. That's the power people give to one another because they want each other to be more powerful—and indispensable, too.

CHAPTER SUMMARY

- Lift people up and they will lift you up, too.

- Focus on the work. When the work goes better, the relationship will go better.

- Too many would-be go-to people emphasize politics, popularity, or even friendship. Instead:

  - Foster authentic rapport by talking about the work you have in common.

  - Build enduring political power at work by being a reliable public servant.

- Take a continuous improvement approach to your number-one asset.

  - Step one: Take time to celebrate success.

    * Make a great thank-you one of your signatures.

  - Step two: Examine and fine-tune your modus operandi.

    * Channel complaining, blaming, and finger-pointing into continuous improvement. Get in the habit of doing after-action reviews.

  - Step three: Plan ahead.

    * End every work interaction or transaction by looking around the corner at the next opportunity to be of service to each other.

- Relationship building is an upward spiral in the making. You can never have too many go-to people or preferred customers.

8

Go-to-ism

The Art of Being Indispensable at Work

Dave Christiansen, who served for decades as president and CEO of Mid-Kansas Coop (MKC), a billion-dollar agricultural cooperative, says he truly grasped the true power of culture while observing employees at Walt Disney World. He loves to tell the following story—a classic example of go-to-ism in action.

On a visit to Walt Disney World, Dave noticed one person in particular, a woman who worked backstage, away from the limelight of the Cinderella Castle, the stage extravaganzas, and elaborate rides. She was a member of the housekeeping staff at a Disney hotel, a difficult and largely invisible role. Yet, despite the hard work and long days, she was smiling through it all.

Dave recalls: "When I asked her how her day was going, she said, 'Great!'" Then she told Dave something remarkable: "She said she had one of the most important jobs on the property."

The reason? "When people go to bed at night," she told Dave, "they turn back their bedclothes, and those crisp sheets and pillowcases are what they fall asleep on. It's the last impression they have of Disney every night."

Dave never forgot how much pride and connection that woman had in her work: "I knew then if I could ever bring that type of culture to any company I lead, it would be transformational. It was and is." He continued to send members of his team to Disney for years for training in customer-service excellence.

Of course, exporting a Disney-level culture to other companies isn't easy. Many leaders have tried and failed to do it. So, what was Dave's secret all those decades? "I always knew that virtually every one of my employees shows up on day one enthusiastic, ready to go to work, and ready to make a difference," he says. "They're looking for someone to emulate whom they respect. They want to know what good work looks like, how they can measure it for themselves, and how *you*—the boss—are going to measure it. They want to know, 'To whom do I make a difference?'"

Dave ensures that each employee understands their importance to MKC, from day one and every day after. "Managers play a pivotal role in building a strong company culture," he says, "but only if they do the hard work of turning vague values into concrete actions employees can take." For example, Dave made driving innovation and creativity part of MKC's culture, and Dave was always sure to help his managers stay focused on that by talking about it and rewarding it.

"We would always look for people who are coaches and teach-ers," he explains. "People who love helping others grow." He would also encourage managers to discover their people's special talents and interests, and to tweak the job description accordingly. "Identify the integral role that individuals play, and help them un-derstand exactly how their contributions will make a difference."

To do that, Dave says, you have to get to know your people. "What are their skills and strengths? Retaining talent is easier when you give them opportunities to demonstrate their skills. Giving people more opportunities for industry involvement and recognition can also make a huge difference." That means of-fering high-potential employees special projects to see how well they perform. "But also give them opportunities to mentor, coach, and meet with other high-potential employees, and chal-lenge them to innovate. That will tell you a lot about what sets them apart."

He continues: "Identify the people who are motivated by the mission and how they contribute to that mission. Then, find out what connects them to their work and tap into that natural mo-tivation whenever possible. Support, guide, and coach them."

That's how Dave fostered go-to-ism at MKC. And he did it because he knows go-to-ism holds the key to working effectively across blurred and crisscrossed lines of accountability.

How can you foster go-to-ism throughout *your* organization?

The Heart of Go-to-ism

I think of go-to-ism as "the way of the go-to person," which re-sults in an upward spiral of mutually reinforcing *real* influence and mutual value-adding in every one of your working relationships. When you have people like that Disney housekeeper at every level of the organization, working behind the scenes and out front, it creates a virtuous cycle. You and your colleagues keep getting better and better at working together.

You might say that go-to-ism is both a philosophy of work and a way of conducting yourself at work. It is a particular way of moving in the world—how you think and what you do. To really buy into the philosophy, you must believe in the peculiar mathematics of real influence. That means playing the long game of serving others—making yourself incredibly valuable to the people around you, building goodwill and a positive reputation. All of which makes others want to do things for you and make good use of your time.

And what about how you conduct yourself? Go-to people don't do everything for everybody or even everything for one particular person. Rather, they approach every relationship determined to add value to every interaction and to every other person. They do no more and no less than what they can do with integrity, working smart and finishing what they start.

Does that mean that anybody and everybody can be a go-to person? I don't see why not. Why would you have an organization—or a team—where anybody is *not* indispensable? Think of it: "Yes, that person works here, but no, you don't want to go to him." It's far better to be able to say, "Oh, yes, *everyone* here is a go-to person. You can go to anyone on my team!" That should be the goal, anyway.

Some teams are created to be just that. Think of them as go-to teams. There's a lot we can learn about fostering a company culture of go-to-ism from teams that are created, from the beginning, to be indispensable.

The Best of the Best

I've had the honor and privilege of working as a researcher, consultant, and trainer for many professionals in the US military, including special operations forces. Think about Army Special Forces (Green Berets), Navy SEALs, Marine Reconnaissance, Air Force Special Operations. These are meant to be the best of the best. These groups are strikingly impressive—their esprit de corps, the powerful ethic of service and sacrifice, the reeking confidence and skill.

What I find most striking about these groups is how much their identity as a group comes precisely *from the fact that they exclude others*. Who they are is *not* everybody else—the people who didn't make it into their special elite group—the non–go-to people.

Selectivity and exclusivity are built into the very DNA of these organizations. Their training and qualification programs require a special application process, with a low acceptance rate. Once accepted, trainees are put through an incredibly rigorous schedule of nonstop physical, mental, and emotional lessons, exercises, and tests.

The SEALs' training is famously difficult; only about one in five make it all the way through. Part of being a SEAL is the fact that very few people can be a SEAL. The SEALs are just one example. Many organizations and teams are, because of their selectivity, exclusivity, or rigor, meant to select out all the non–go-to people. Think of Harvard University, any state bar association, almost any medical school, the major leagues of any sport, the GE Audit program. Think of McKinsey, which has among the most coveted and powerful consulting jobs anybody graduating from, say, Harvard, can hope to get. Think Enterprise Rent-A-Car, in which new employees are brought further and further on board (or not) with a 30-day test, a 60-day test, a 90-day test, and finally after 180 days, a test it used to call "the grill."

It is often said about such elite organizations, "The hardest part is getting in." Indeed, part of the idea is that, when you're in such an elite group, you are in such very good company. It takes continued excellence to stay in, make no mistake. But, it's that much easier to continue succeeding at such a high level in a group where there are no low performers whose gaps must be covered. Everybody is operating at such a high level, already above and beyond, that every member of the team inspires and assists the others in staying at that level every step of the way.

Once you are part of such a group, you will ever after have the imprimatur, not to mention the knowledge, skill, experience, relationships, and muscle memory of operating at that level with that level of people. This will serve you during your entire life and career.

So, if you are part of one of these elite groups, you know that it's possible to build a culture intentionally around go-to-ism, a culture in which everybody is expected to be indispensable. That makes it a lot easier to succeed.

If you are part of a culture that isn't elite and doesn't particularly appreciate go-to people, take confidence from the examples I've just named: know that elite cultures are something that can be created *intentionally*.

Someone Always Rises to the Top of the Best

Being elite is all relative. Even within the most elite group, there is always the elite within the elite: the go-to people's go-to person. You would choose that person to go to *first*, even within an elite group. Usually that person is the most reliable, the one who helps others get their needs met, on spec, on time, with minimal stress—every time. That person always brings their best to the table and brings out the best in others.

Why shouldn't that person be you? If you are part of an elite group, three cheers. Bank everything you can from that experience. It sure makes it easier to perform at a high level when the culture supports that, because that's what the culture is all about. Still, within that elite culture, where are you? In the front guard or the rear? Why not shoot for being the elite within the elite? Be the go-to person on the go-to team. Whatever you do, do it very well, very fast, all day long, with a great attitude. Think about Lisa Wolf, the nurse in the emergency room (chapter 2). Because the stakes are so high, the ER workers had to be an elite group. But Lisa rose above them all by being the person who was aligned up, down, sideways, and diagonally. The person who was known for great judgment and for going above and beyond, every chance she got. She was the nurse everyone wanted to work with, the go-to team's go-to person. (See the sidebar on a related topic, "A Network? Or a Clique?")

What If Your Culture Doesn't Support Go-to-ism?

If you do not happen to be a Navy SEAL and you're not part of some other elite group within your organization, how can you

A Network? Or a Clique?

Go-to people by their very nature tend to be an exclusive bunch. They naturally network with one another and offer mutual support. Unfortunately, that means cliques sometimes emerge in the workplace and wreak havoc. That can happen when:

- Inclusion or exclusion is based on personal factors rather than business.

- People within the group are unwilling to support those outside the group.

- People within the group are unwilling to seek support from those outside the group.

But even when there is nothing about the group or individuals that excludes others *intentionally*, sometimes people feel excluded nevertheless. One group of five people in a marketing team at a financial services firm regularly went to lunch together. The problem was that this group never invited anyone else to join them for lunch. Within the department, people began to feel excluded and quickly formed the perception that this group within marketing was a clique, which bred unnecessary bad will.

You might say, "Hold on just a minute. What's wrong with networking, bonding over team lunches, or even meeting regularly with a group with whom you have a lot in common? After all, there's a lot of power in esprit de corps, in being part of a supportive group of people who want to lift each other up."

That's true. So, within your own group or network, how do you avoid the negative aspects of exclusivity that can veer into cliquishness? Consider two guidelines.

Welcome Whoever Shows Up and Delivers

When I was growing up, my family lived two doors from a man named David Katz. He was the father of two of my best friends, and he was a classic go-to person—a great citizen, neighbor, parent, friend, you name it. David was always ready to carry more than his own weight and to encourage others to do so as well.

When David died too young, in 1998, my family was there when his coffin was lowered into his grave. Jewish people have a tradition of burying their own, so one by one, people stepped up to throw in some dirt. Eventually it was time to fill in the grave, so David's children and close friends took up the shovels that had been placed by the dirt pile next to the grave.

I just stood there motionless, tears in my eyes, not sure if I should include myself in this elite group. Suddenly, I heard David in my own head, saying, "Come on, Bruce. Grab a shovel! Do your part." As soon as I picked up the shovel, I knew I belonged.

I've heard similar stories from network leaders in organizations. One told me, "Well, if this is my clique, then at least I can promise you one thing: everybody is welcome in this clique as long as you carry your own weight. The more the merrier. Show up and deliver."

Should everybody be welcome in your circle or network of go-to people? I submit that they should—as long as they're willing to grab a shovel and do their part.

Diversify and Cross-Pollinate

One informal network leader told me, "I don't know if ours is an exclusive clique. If it is, then fine. But *I'm* not exclusive to this clique, that's for sure. I am diversified and cross-pollinated. I want to be a valuable contributor of every clique that is worth being part of, and I'm happy to introduce anyone to anyone."

That's what go-to-ism really is all about: be a go-to person. Find go-to people wherever you need them. And build new go-to people whenever you have the chance.

After all, "indispensable" is in the eye of the beholder. Indispensable to whom? To as many people as possible, especially preferred customers and other go-to people. Make yourself super valuable to as many people as you can. Diversify and cross-pollinate. And upward the spiral goes.

hope to operate at a high level? After all, some companies simply lack the resources to support a high level of performance. They don't have the choice of top talent, the selection process, the training assets, or the coaching-style leadership that would allow the organization to create an elite, elite corps. So, you might feel that any go-to-ism on your part would leave you swimming against a strong current.

Or you might be facing some other problem that discourages you from being a go-to person. What if your organization has a bunch of low performers who always cause problems? They continually make messes that the high performers spend all their time fixing—time that could be channeled into developing as go-to people. Or the low performers see you working double time, and they resent it. They might even be saying, "Hey, slow down. You're making me look bad." In some cultures, the problem is simply that there's no special reward for operating at a higher level.

The good news about not being part of an elite team or organization (like the SEALs) is that it is easier for you to stand out among the others and even rise to the top. No matter where you work or what you do, if you conduct yourself as a go-to person, you are the person who is always adding value, always trying to serve others, always trying to do great work and be great to work with. That's going to make things better for you and others in your sphere of influence.

Sometimes people say, "But it doesn't feel fair. And maybe it isn't even wise to be indispensable. I will be doing much more than my share, with no special reward. And I might even be punished for it by the low performers."

Don't take your cues from people like that. Anybody who is saying, "Slow down, you're making me look bad," shouldn't be your role model. You have to believe in the peculiar mathematics of real influence. By serving others, you build up your value and your reputation, immediately and for the long term. Even where there are naysayers or mean-spirited low performers, there have to be at least *some* people who see the good you're doing and appreciate it. By adding value, you make the entire enterprise more valuable for everyone, including you. Remember? The math is peculiar.

So even if you are the sole go-to person among a sea of losers, better to be that solitary indispensable employee than to be dragging your heels. It's better for you, because you're always doing your personal best. And it's better for the people around you, because you might just raise the bar.

If you look out over the landscape and for miles and miles you're the only go-to person in sight, I predict one of three things will happen:

1. The whole enterprise will fizzle sooner or later, but you will learn and grow from the experience instead of wasting your time and energy as a low performer.

2. You will rise to the top and become a leader in your department or organization.

3. You will quickly discover (and this is what I believe is most likely) that you aren't the only go-to person in a sea of losers. By making yourself indispensable, you'll draw out other like-minded folks, and you'll start a movement within the enterprise. Go-to people are like magnets who attract each other.

So, while you might not be part of the Navy SEALs, it is still very unlikely that there are literally *no* go-to people in your organization except you. Indeed, you'll probably discover there are more potentially extraordinary people there than you'd imagined.

When you bring your best to the table, no matter where you are or what you are doing, you bring out the best in others. And soon, you start to realize, that, in turn, helps them bring out the best in you.

That's the upward spiral. You find each other and form an elite group of go-to people in an otherwise ordinary context. I see that happen everywhere I go: circles or networks of go-to people who help each other and go out of their way to be mutually reliable.

Sometimes it takes the form of a team or project. Or it could be a loose confederation of people who need each other and agree, formally or informally, to support each other. I saw that happen in one nonprofit I worked with, where a small cadre of like-minded people formed their own kind of continuous improvement co-alition. Made up of individuals from different departments, the coalition initially met to brainstorm about new projects, but in-evitably they all became go-to people for each other. (For another example, see the sidebar "When Go-to-ism Becomes Infectious.")

Building the Upward Spiral

Go-to-ism describes an essential belief: that serving others very well is what being indispensable is all about. The greatest source of social power—real influence—comes from being a person others want to go to in order to get their needs met. Serving others is what makes you the kind of person others want to help succeed. This is not an exchange, but rather the outcome of others respecting who you are and how you conduct yourself. As a result of your real influence, others want you to be powerful because your power helps them get their needs met and poten-tially makes them more powerful, too.

That's how you build the upward spiral. Sometimes, at this point, people stop me and say, "Wait. You are building an 'upward

When Go-to-ism Becomes Infectious

Sometimes the gravitational pull of a loose confederation of go-to people becomes infectious, and there is nowhere to hide.

That's what happened at one mid-level restaurant chain that was struggling at the corporate level, closing one location after another, and heading toward eventual bankruptcy. In the midst of all that, a few individual restaurants were defying the trend in key indicators. Their guest counts were still good, as were their per-guest gross revenues and customer-service ratings. Employee turnover was relatively low. One restaurant in particular was truly thriving.

What accounted for the unusual success of those restaurants? There were no obvious factors, such as favorable location, and they worked under the same constraints as the other stores did: limited budgets for labor, advertising, food, and so on. I decided to investigate. This was just the sort of anomaly that is central to our research.

What were they doing that the others were not? Nothing at all, as it turned out. They were just doing *more of it and doing it better.* How? After looking for explanations in every corner, I concluded that, as individual store teams, they were simply trying harder—at the work and at working together. And it was contagious. True, each of those restaurants enjoyed the leadership of a great general manager (GM)—hardworking, smart-working, upbeat, highly engaged in every direction—quintessential go-to people.

But more than that, a team of go-to people had grown up around each of those GMs, which in turn bred a culture of go-to-ism. Each successful outlier shared an esprit de corps and a determination to succeed that fed on itself; people wanted to go the extra mile because they saw others going the extra mile. They might as well have been a special operations team.

I asked one assistant manager about his restaurant's success. He said that for a while, they'd been plagued by a revolving door of new employees. The new hires sapped the labor budget, needed training, and in the end often were of little help. "We started out as a small core group," he told me. "We basically told [our GM], please let us work more. We will work more hours, work harder, work multiple roles, whatever."

Their plan was a success, and the store's numbers improved. "We all are fully aware the company still might go out of business," he added. "But I think we will all look back and be proud to have been part of this team."

spiral' of go-to people and preferred customers and, for many of them, you are also a go-to person. You are all connected and super valuable to each other. Is this just old-fashioned 'networking' by another name?"

They're right, of course. But I hesitate to use the word "networking" because it sometimes evokes negative connotations. People tell me, "I hate networking." Strangely, these are often go-to people themselves with their own preferred customers. And they are the preferred customers for their own go-to people. They have these great upward-spiraling networks, but they think they hate networking.

Why? Networking, per se, seems to imply a relationship orientation where you focus on using other people to get your needs met. You socialize, but you're really hoping to get some professional benefit, maybe partly for reasons of personal affinity or organizational politics. Or maybe you do professional favors in hopes of receiving similar favors.

But that view of networking actually describes something else entirely. It describes *false influence* thinking, which we explored in depth earlier in the book: "How can I use my 'influence' (flattery, bribery, or threats) to get what I need from you?" No wonder so many people think they hate networking.

People who try to network using false influence usually have very little real influence, because using false influence is often transparent and such a turnoff to most people. Conversely, people who build up real influence over time are those who approach relationships, even networking, from exactly the opposite point of view: "What can I do for you?" Rather than seeing other people's needs as a burden, go-to people see others' needs as an opportunity to add value and, as a result, become more valuable themselves. Instead of weighing you down, others' needs actually lift you up.

Build that upward spiral by:

1. Being a go-to person

2. Finding go-to people wherever you need them—and then being their most amazing customer

3. Building up new go-to people whenever you have the chance

Be a Go-to Person

At the beginning of this book, I laid out some of the table stakes of being a go-to person. Go-to people:

- Make themselves valuable to others

- Maintain a positive attitude, an attitude of service

- Double down on hard work

- Are good at their jobs

- Are creative and tenacious

- Take personal responsibility for getting things done

The rest of this book has, I hope, spelled out for you that there's so much more to being a go-to person. They:

- Believe in the peculiar mathematics of real influence

- Lead from wherever they are by aligning themselves up, down, sideways, and diagonally

- Know when to say no and how to say yes

- Work smart and finish what they start

- Keep getting better and better at working together

Doing all of this consistently is the only way to stay ahead of overcommitment syndrome—which, of course, is the only way to do all of this consistently.

Meanwhile, you cannot afford to be the only go-to person at work, and why would you want to be? It's not enough to be a go-to person yourself. So, be sure that you:

- Find go-to people wherever you need them

- Build up new go-to people whenever you have the chance

The rest of this book is about building up your working relationships, one by one, systematically constructing that upward spiral of real influence: the power that people give each other because they want each other to be powerful.

Find Go-to People and Be Their Most Amazing Customer

Many of your own preferred customers will also become your go-to people. But that doesn't mean you stop being of service. Whenever you find go-to people, you still want to approach those relationships with a service mindset. So, when *you* are the customer, what do you bring to those relationships? The ability to be a great customer, of course. Here's how.

Rule One: Learn who's who in the zoo. I learned that rule from Mary Trout, mentioned in chapter 6 (GSD), who, I will add, is one of my favorite CEOs in the making and, obviously, a total go-to person. "You have to learn who's who in the zoo," she says. That is, who are the teddy bears? The tigers? The snakes? Get to know the players in all the different areas of the organization—up, down, sideways, and diagonal—their strengths and weaknesses, their work proclivities, and how to work effectively with them. Figure out how to find your go-to people and how to get what you need from them.

That's doubly important if you are relatively new in an organization, especially one with a long history and lots of long-standing personnel and internal networks, or if you are one of the long-standing personnel in an organization that is now bringing in more and more new blood.

Rule Two: Start with the people you know. If you start with people you don't know, then you have to get to know them and figure out if you have reason to trust them. If you start with the people you know already, you can zero in on those you trust to find your go-to people.

Start with your own best customers. You should always be looking around the corner with them, anticipating upcoming opportunities to be of service to each other. Which of your own best customers might be go-to people for you? Do you know enough about their world?

You already know what you can do for them, how they operate, and how to do business with them. Do you know what they can do for you? Where do their tasks, responsibilities, and projects meet up with your needs?

Give them opportunities to add value. And then be an amazing customer for them (see Rule Five).

Rule Three: Study the hall files. Your go-to go-to person may not always be available. Or maybe the people you know best don't do exactly what you need.

But maybe they know somebody who does. Ask your go-to people for referrals. And use your extended network, too. You might get the name of someone's friend of a friend. It's someplace to start. You can always get a second opinion about the person, and a third. Shop around a little. Find someone who really delivers.

Referrals and second and third opinions are all ways into the personnel "hall files." Everybody has a hall file—their informal reputation. This is what people who have worked with them whisper about them in the halls. The good and the not so good. This is informal reputation data held in the opinions that colleagues have about each other. Consider the hall file just another repository of real influence.

Some people have a hall file that says, "This person does such great work and is so great to work with: you want to work with this person." Others have a hall file that says, "You don't want to work with this person." Some are full of stories and examples. Others are vague. Be careful how you use hall-file data, but don't ignore it. Even when it sinks to the level of gossip, never forget that gossip is data, too—but also remember it isn't always true.

Ask around. You'll learn a lot. And don't believe everything you hear. Get second and third opinions.

Rule Four: Study the organization chart. Finally, when all else fails, you can always use the organization charts and employee directories. I'm amazed at how many organizations have great charts and directories that are up to date and available to personnel, but that few people access and utilize.

To find go-to people where you need them, you need to know exactly who's who in the organization and who exactly to go to for what, why, how, where, or when. So study the org chart. Study the employee directories. Learn who does what, why, when, where, and how. Make the connections. And keep up with the changes.

Rule Five: Be an amazing customer. Once you find your go-to people, be their most amazing customer. What does that mean? First, you give your go-to people a lot of business—your own and through your referrals and recommendations. Maybe the amazing customer sometimes overtips or errs on the high side when it comes to discretionary contingent pay and other rewards. But does an amazing customer overpay? No. Unless the relationship is somehow corrupt, the amazing customer pays a fair price.

But there's a lot more to being a great customer than giving somebody your business and paying good money. You also give them positive word of mouth, business referrals, comfort, ease, and trust in dealings. And who knows? The person selling (or helping you with) something today could be *your* customer tomorrow, or your boss, your direct report, colleague, teacher, friend, or uncle-in-law.

And because great customers have a lot of offer, they get a lot back. Great customers get all the best deals, the free samples, the speedy deliveries, the emergency rush jobs on a weekend or holiday. Why? The best customers are also great to work with. That doesn't just mean just being polite and familiar. It means that you:

- Go to the right person about the right things at the right time (hint: with plenty of advance notice).

- Go prepared and make good use of the other person's time.

- Go vertical first and check for alignment, so you don't have to come back later and say, "My boss said we have to make this change" or "My direct reports/my team says we have to make this change."

- Tune in to your own ask: put your asks in the form of a tight proposal.

- Answer the "no gate" questions on the way in:

    - Yes, it can be done; it's possible.

    - Yes, it is allowed.

    - Yes, it should be done; it has good ROI.

- Make yes easy by setting out a simple plan: here's how I will help you help me.

- Always follow up and build the relationship: send a supersonic thank-you. Do an after-action review. And look around the corner so you can plan the next collaboration.

If you can do all of the things I've described so far in this section, the final building block in this upward spiral should come more easily to you.

Build Up New Go-to People Whenever You Have the Chance

Every day I tell people that a big part of go-to-ism is going out of your way to find high-potential individuals at every level in all parts of the organization. And then you invest some of your own time and energy in building them up.

The first most-common reaction I hear is: "Great idea, but who has time for that?" The second reaction is: "Yes, but I'm not qualified and it's not my place." The third: "It's 'dog eat dog' out here. Why should I spend my time helping someone else do their job and build up their career?"

If you have gotten this far in this book and you are still having that third "dog eat dog" reaction, then I obviously haven't reached you. Why are you still reading this book?

Go-to people are worth every ounce of time and effort. You cannot accomplish much without them. And you can never have too many go-to people—in your orbit, on your team, in your organization. As to the first and second most-common reactions: actually, you do not have time *not* to do that; and you don't need any qualifications to help other people get better.

I am not saying that you need to dedicate yourself to becoming a personal or professional coach for your colleagues or, even, for your direct reports (although you owe them some amount of coaching). But why not try to help people you work with get better as a result of working with you? What can you help this person get better at, just from working with you? Anything? At the very least, every time you work with somebody, help that person get better at working better with you.

It is your place. Help people get better. Any time you help anybody at work get better at anything, you are building additional productive capacity in that person that will keep adding value every time that person does that thing (or something similar) going forward.

If you are anybody's boss, part of your job is helping your people get better. You owe it to them to be a coaching-style or teaching-style leader: spelling out expectations at every step; following up; guiding, directing, supporting; tracking performance; troubleshooting; problem solving; and providing course-correcting feedback.

What are you doing to build up your direct reports? What about those who want to be go-to people but are really struggling? Try helping them get better at their jobs and to go the extra mile. Teach them how to work faster, smarter, and finish what they start. Show them by example how to do those things with a better attitude. Encourage them to learn and grow and aim for the next level.

If you want a team of go-to people, that means being very honest and very ruthless. Help every single person get better and better. But you cannot tolerate stubborn low performers on your team. They are a waste of money. They cause problems that others have to fix. High performers hate dealing with them. And they send a message that low performance may be an option.

Once you commit to a "no low performers" rule, then you can help every person on the team get better and become more of a go-to person—one person at a time, one day at a time.

You don't have to be the boss to help people get better. No matter where you are in the organization chart, you can set a great example by how you work and how you work with others. Be the kind of coworker others want to emulate and imitate.

Understand that helping others get better will work to your benefit. When you build someone up, usually that person will never forget what you've done for them. Many of them will go out into the world and be successful. Who knows all the ways you may be able to help each other in the future?

When you build up other people, you build a reputation for fostering them, as opposed to someone who has a reputation for tearing down others. When you have a reputation for building up other people, they tend to root for you. Why wouldn't they?

Put together, all of these things add up to go-to-ism. That's the art of being indispensable.

Spread the Word . . . or Keep It a Secret . . . but You Won't Be Able To

Whether you are an individual trying to navigate the gig economy or a foot soldier in the collaboration revolution, go-to-ism will make you more effective, saner, and happier.

The business value of go-to-ism? Effectively push as much communication, decision making, and cooperative action as far down the chain of command as possible. Align in every direction and empower individuals so they can work smart and finish what they start. When it works well, everything runs more smoothly and swiftly: information exchange, decision making, planning, resource sharing, and execution. It also reduces unnecessary problems and waste.

The value to you? You will get more of the right work done, better and faster, win real influence at every step, and beat overcommitment in the process.

If you've read this book and can see how powerful this approach is, you might think this can be your secret weapon of indispensability. You might be tempted to keep these new ideas and habits to yourself, to help give you a strategic advantage. Go ahead and try, but you probably won't be able to.

Because people *will* notice and ask, "What is it you're doing? You are getting so much done, so much faster and better, but you seem to have so much more control over your time, your assignments, and so much more choice over who you are working with. Everybody seems to want to work with you. What gives?"

You could try to keep it a secret, just among you and your primary collaborators. And maybe that would give you and your growing network of preferred customers an advantage, at least for a while.

But then others will notice even more. People will keep asking. Word is going to spread. More people you work with will start following your example and the example of your growing network. And that helps create more go-to people and makes your work easier and better.

Why would you *want* to keep it a secret? Go-to-ism could start to redefine the culture of your team, your department, maybe even your whole company. It could spread to your home life and your family and friends. Soon the goodwill and virtuous cycle of go-to-ism could start jumping across state lines.

Who knows? Go-to-ism could become a movement.

Index

Acknowledgments

Thanks to all the indispensable go-to people everywhere whom I've had the privilege to know, including so very many who are not mentioned herein.

In particular, thanks to the following:

The more than half-a-million incredible individuals from over four hundred organizations who have participated in our survey, interview, and focus group research since 1993. Thanks also to the many leaders in business, nonprofit, and government organizations who have expressed such confidence in our work by hiring us to conduct assessments, provide advice, and run training programs.

To all those people who have attended my keynotes and seminars over the years: thanks for listening, laughing, sharing the wisdom of your experience, pushing me with the really tough questions, being kind, and teaching me. My greatest intellectual debt is to all of these real people in the real world who have allowed me to help them wrestle with their challenges. Special thanks to those whose stories appear in this book. I've only named a few individuals; for the most part, I have used pseudonyms and I've also mixed up the ancillary details to help keep the stories anonymous.

To my colleagues past and present at RainmakerThinking, especially the current team—Kimberli Math, Elizabeth

("Lightning Girl") Richards, and Cheryl Wolansky—thank you for your real-influence thinking, alignment, good decisions, smart work, valuable contributions, and commitment to getting better at working together every step of the way. Every one of you is a true go-to person. I consider each of you to be a true friend, and I am deeply grateful for the opportunity to work with you all.

If you have never visited the RainmakerThinking offices next door to my house in Whitneyville, Connecticut, you might not know that in the same house where the business is located is our dojo, where we practice karate. Also living there is my life-long karate teacher (since I was seven years old), the great Master Frank Gorman, about whom I've written in other books: he's the "Karate Master Next Door" in the situation comedy I'm writing in my head. And, also, Frank's grandson, my honorary nephew, dear friend, and karate student Nathan Gorman. And, also, Nathan's dog, Bentley Kanbun Gorman, who is now among my newest and best of friends. All three Gormans are family. I have bent all of their ears about this book for years now. Frank, an avid reader, has read several earlier drafts and made suggestions. Nathan has listened patiently on many a car ride and made suggestions. And Bentley has listened kindly but entirely without comment. I am grateful to all of them.

When it comes to karate, I could thank everybody with whom I've ever trained, as I wouldn't be the same without them all. I must thank the current primary members of my own dojo, in addition to Frank and Nathan and Bentley: Ian Sweeney (who is married to Lightning Girl) and Charles Jones, along with lifelong dojo members Rob Schulman, Michael Harrigan, Joe Gilbert, Ryan Dean, Bob Misseau, Chris Cox, Peggy Hess, Geoff Crouse, and Sam Malissa, as well as Bob Kaiser (who gave me the story about the dentist lawyer Eric Ploumis). Geoff (whom I've known since 1983), the "Karate Master CEO" in the memoir I'm writing, has been one of my best clients, as well as one of my best friends and also, other than Frank, my primary teacher in the dojo. He's a great source of wisdom and is quoted in this book. Sam, also a very close friend, has been my karate student since 2012 and worked with us at RainmakerThinking (2018–2020). Sam and I had many conversations about early iterations of the book, and he read and made very helpful comments on the first draft.

Pamela Haag, not a karateka, but also a very close friend and a brilliant writer, editor, and scholar in her own right, came to Whitneyville early in my writing process (spring 2019) and spent a long weekend with me and a laptop, asking questions, typing notes, and lending her advice and support. Pam's patience, insight, and guidance were critical to the early formation of the book and well worth every minute and every penny.

Two more of my very oldest and closest friends, Steve Katz (my oldest friend, tied with his twin brother Jeff; and sons of David Katz, mentioned in chapter 8) and Lisa Wolf (from Amherst days). Both Steve and Lisa read and commented at length on the first draft. They both gave me excellent advice that I incorporated almost in entirety. Indeed, my conversation with Lisa made me realize she was the perfect character with whom to open chapter 2.

And then there is Harvard Business Review Press. I have had some great publishers over the years. But I've always coveted HBR Press and always wanted to publish a book with it. I am profoundly thankful to Melinda Merino, editorial director, and Jeff Kehoe, executive editor, for believing in this book and throwing their weight and prestige behind it. Thanks to the whole team at Harvard including Sally Ashworth, Julie Devoll, Lindsey Dietrich, Alexandra Kephart, Erika Heilman, Jon Shipley, Felicia Sinusas, and Alicyn Zall. Thank you all, from the bottom of my heart, for the honor of working with you and HBR Press. I hope I've lived up to your confidence in me.

Jeff Kehoe gave me lots of support and encouragement along the way and great feedback on the first draft, making extensive notes on the initial manuscript, giving me a chance to bring the manuscript up a whole level, and then giving me a very smart piece of advice/marching order: "You can take this manuscript to yet another new level by working with the go-to person of developmental editors, the very talented, diligent, and effective Lucy McCauley." Being a good soldier, I worked with Lucy McCauley, who has taken a scalpel to this manuscript and a paintbrush and clay and ribbons and frosting. She helped me add so much valuable structure and substance from the first page to the last. Thank you, Lucy, so very much for your spectacular work. This book is so much better because of you.

Meanwhile, Susan Rabiner, my agent (also my wife Debby's agent) and our dear friend, is always there behind the scenes of our careers in book publishing. Susan is otherworldly when it comes to understanding books and setting them up for success. Talk about knowing when to say no and how to say yes. Susan is truly a genius when it comes to helping a writer figure out whether and how to turn an idea into a book worth publishing. Genius Susan and her genius husband, the late Al Fortunato, wrote the book on publishing nonfiction, *Thinking Like Your Editor*. Susan talked me through every stage of turning my latest research into this book.

To my family and friends, I owe my deep and abiding thanks for allowing me to be me and for being who you are. Thanks to my parents, Henry and Norma Tulgan (d. 2016); my parents-in-law, Julie and Paul Applegate; my nieces and nephews (from youngest to oldest): Eli, Frances, Erin, Perry, and Elisa; my sister, Ronna, and my brother, Jim; my sister-in-law, Tanya, and my brothers-in-law, Shan and Tom, and Jim's life partner, Debbie (and their grandson, Emerson). I love every one of you so very much.

I should add a special thanks to my sister, Ronna, who read an early outline and also the first full draft of the book, gave me great comments on both, and had several very helpful conversations with me along the way. (She did the same thing, I recall, way back in the early nineties on my very first book, *Managing Generation X*.) Thanks Ronna!

Special thanks to my ever-loving parents for all that hard work of raising me and for being among the very most supportive parents and closest friends I could ever hope for. I treasure every single minute we have spent together. This is my first book since losing my mother, which makes me feel very sad. But this book is dedicated to my father, which makes me feel very happy.

Also special thanks to Frances, who since the age of five minutes has been the closest I've ever had to my own child. Fran, I will never be your father, but you will always be my daughter.

Finally, I reserve my most profound thanks always for my wife, Dr. Debby Applegate, winner of the 2007 Pulitzer Prize for Biography for her book *The Most Famous Man in America: The Biography of Henry Ward Beecher* and author of the forthcoming *Madam: The Notorious Life and Times of Polly Adler*. Debby's books (and articles) are so good, such fine specimens of writing and thinking; she is my beacon of inspiration whenever I'm writing or thinking.

She asks the toughest questions and offers the most interesting answers. She has literally and literarily held my hand throughout the writing of this book and, really, through every move I've made over the last (nearly) thirty-five years. I asked Debby to marry me when she was seventeen. It took me eight years to convince her. And here we are. Debby is my constant adviser, my greatest supporter, my toughest critic, my closest collaborator, the love of my life, my best friend, my smartest friend, my partner in all things, half of my soul, owner of my heart, and the person without whom I would cease to be. Thank you, my love.

About the Author

BRUCE TULGAN is an adviser to business leaders all over the world and a sought-after keynote speaker, seminar leader, and consultant. He is the founder of RainmakerThinking, Inc., a workplace research and training firm. Bruce is the author of the bestseller *It's Okay to Be the Boss*, the classic *Managing Generation X, Not Everyone Gets a Trophy*, and *The 27 Challenges Managers Face*, as well as many other books. More than a half-million individuals from more than four hundred organizations have participated in Bruce's research since 1993, and his work has been the subject of thousands of news stories worldwide. He has written pieces for numerous publications, including the *New York Times, USA Today, Harvard Business Review, TD, Training*, and *Human Resources*. Bruce holds a sixth-degree black belt in classical Okinawan Uechi Ryu karate, making him a master in that style. His wife, Debby Applegate, PhD, won the 2007 Pulitzer Prize for Biography for her book *The Most Famous Man in America* and is also the author of the forthcoming *Madam*. They live together in Whitneyville, Connecticut. Bruce can be reached on twitter @brucetulgan or by email at brucet@rainmakerthinking.com.

When you *Know* *yourself* = ~~Emp~~.
= Empowered

When you *accept* *yourself*
= You become Invinceable